The Escape of the Goeben

Also by Redmond McLaughlin
THE ROYAL ARMY MEDICAL CORPS

The Escape of the Goeben

PRELUDE TO GALLIPOLI

'No part of the Great War compares with its opening ... the first collision was a drama never surpassed.'

WINSTON CHURCHILL

by
Redmond McLaughlin

Charles Scribner's Sons
New York

940.454

MCLAUGHLIN

1 3 5 7 9 11 13 15 17 19 I/C 20 18 16 14 12 10 8 6 4 2

Library of Congress Catalog Card Number 73-190 94
SBN 684-13761-5

Printed in Great Britain

Dedicated by permission to
Professor Arthur J. Marder
Prince of naval historians
and forthright friend of the
Royal Navy

CONTENTS

ILLUSTRATIONS

ACKNOWLEDGEMENTS

Any landsman who embarks on the stormy waters of naval history and attempts to analyse a highly controversial episode must stand in need of expert navigation. If he is lucky he will finally owe, as I do, a massive debt to many people for their kindly help and advice.

My first thanks are due to Her Majesty the Queen for her gracious permission to use a letter in the Royal Archives quoted by Professor Marder; also to Miss Jane Langton, the Windsor Registrar, for her kindness in establishing that, surprisingly, there are no papers in the Archives referring to any aspect of the *Goeben* affair.

A number of friends and generous strangers earned my gratitude in various ways: these include Captain Eric Bush RN, for much stimulating discussion on Gallipoli and other related topics; Captain Stephen Roskill RN, for an illuminating comment; Commander Sir Richard Colville RN, for leave to quote from a number of letters written by his father, Admiral the Hon. Sir Stanley Colville, Air Marshal Sir Ralph Sorley, for an unexpected anecdote; Mr. Alan James of the U.S. Embassy in London and Herr Hans von Mohl, formerly of SMS *Breslau*.

I have been well served by two Libraries: the Admiralty Library at Earl's Court; and the Library of the Royal United Services Institute where Mr. Dineen and Miss Glover went to great trouble to produce a copy (possibly the only one in this country) of Admiral Souchon's memoirs. This was finally obtained on loan in a French version through the outstanding co-operation of the Musée de la Marine in Paris, and its Director, Monsieur Bayle.

The problem of gaining information on Turkish matters was generously eased by Mr. Michael Warr, formerly H.M. Consul-General at Istanbul; by Mr. John Hyde, the Information Officer at the Consulate General; by the gift of several photographs from the Hayat Agency; and by Mr. Peter Liddle, who saw the *Yavuz* in July 1972; he generously lent me letters from two German sailors and also for copying his remarkable film of Gallipoli. including *Yavuz*.

My special debt is to the late Captain John Creswell RN, the naval historian, and to Rear-Admiral Ian McLaughlan, lately Admiral Commanding Reserves, who read my manuscript with kindly precision and made invaluable comments. My third 'reader' (at quite a different level) was my daughter Elizabeth who disclosed an unexpected talent for spotting tiresome repetitions and clumsy constructions.

I am grateful to the following publishers and authors (or owners of copyright): Jonathan Cape for *Fear God and Dread Nought* by Professor Arthur J. Marder; the Oxford University Press for Marder's *From the Dreadnought to Scapa Flow*; The Hamlyn Group for *The World Crisis* by (Sir) Winston Churchill; Messrs Hutchinson for *My Naval Career* by Admiral Sir Sydney Fremantle, and *Two Lone Ships* by Georg Kopp and in particular to The Navy Records Society and its Secretary, the Hon. David Erskine for *The Mediterranean 1912–14*, edited by E. W. R. Lumby.

The Trustees of the National Maritime Museum, Greenwich, kindly allowed me to use the *Milne Papers*; they also gave me access to the *Troubridge Papers*; for permission to quote from these, and to reproduce a facsimile of two letters to Admiral Sir Ernest Troubridge, I am greatly obliged to his grandson Lieutenant-Commander Sir Peter Troubridge RN, who also lent me two unpublished family photographs. Other photographs are reproduced by courtesy of Mrs Daniel Gurney, the Hayat Agency, the Imperial War Museum, the National Portrait Gallery and the Radio-Hulton Library. Expert resuscitation was needed on some of these, and this was kindly arranged by my colleague, Mr Broadbury.

I was notably fortunate in the two ladies, Mrs Joanna Wilson and Mrs Coral Beddard, who not only typed and retyped my various drafts, but also cheered me up when the going was tough. For, as Sir Basil Liddell Hart has put it: 'Writing history *is* a very tough job—and one of the most exhausting'.

My final debt is to Professor Arthur J. Marder, the supreme authority on the Royal Navy of 1904 to 1918. Like most recent writers in this field my obligations to him are enormous; but he has also been good enough to allow a short book by a stranger to be dedicated to him. Even American generosity could hardly go further.

Introduction

We went on up the narrow strait, anxiously. On this side lay Scylla, and on that the terrible whirlpool of Charybdis.

HOMER'S ODYSSEY

At 10.30 am on 4 August, 1914, just over twelve hours before the British ultimatum to Germany expired, a remarkable and fortuitous encounter took place some 300 miles west of Malta. Two German ships, one of exceptional size, armour, speed and armament, with her small consort, were met on precisely opposite courses by two of Britain's modern battle cruisers. The Germans, already at war with France, had been effectively bombarding two North African ports where French troop convoys were assembling. They were now returning eastwards to neutral Messina. The British were in hot pursuit of an enemy that they envisaged as likely to escape westwards into the Atlantic. The hostile pairs approached each other at a combined speed of about 40 knots (or, in landsman's terms, 47 mph). For a few seconds the future of their two countries, not yet at war, hung in the balance. A momentary failure of nerve or an excess of zeal could have started a fierce battle at close range from which the British, with a vast preponderance of firepower, could hardly have failed to emerge as victors. The courtesy of a formal salute might have triggered off the heavy guns. But at 8,000 yards it was seen that neither leading ship was flying an admiral's flag. All guns, though fully manned, remained trained fore and aft; and the moment of destiny passed—forever.

This book is about the events, political as well as naval—for the two are inextricably linked—that preceded and followed this remarkable encounter.

This remains one of the most significant and fascinating episodes of the Great War. A single German capital ship with one small consort eluded fifteen Allied capital ships, breaking through from the Adriatic to Algeria, and back via Messina to the Dardanelles—and on to Constantinople. As a consequence, Turkey was encouraged in due course to make her shaky entry into the war on Germany's side.

A secondary outcome was the Court Martial, on a charge of negligence, of a British admiral who bore an honoured name. Very recently a full verbatim account of the court proceedings has been released, though not to a general readership. For such publication there are few, if any, precedents. It discloses the detailed charges, allegations and explanations—with a full complement of red herrings. It was a legal confrontation without parallel in this century . . . the dramatic coda to an episode of gallantry, muddle, luck and disaster in waters that had been the setting for the epic of the Odyssey.

1

The Road Towards War

'The naval rivalry did not cause the war, but it ensured that when the war did break out, Great Britain would be on the side of Germany's enemies.' MARDER

THE Diamond Jubilee of 1897 had been an appropriate stage for an impressive Naval Review; and this particular year will serve as a useful starting point for a review of the road towards war at sea in 1914.

Ever since Trafalgar the Royal Navy had enjoyed a prestige that had been earned by a combination of hardihood, pertinacity, seamanship—and sheer genius; and it had remained unchallenged for most of a century. The unnecessary war of 1812 against the former American Colonies came finally to an end in the same year, 1815, as Waterloo.

Since that date any potential Nelsons had been denied participation in a great naval battle. For the next hundred years the effective function of the Navy, apart from odd gunboat incursions, had been occasionally to bombard hostile forts in the Crimea or the Baltic, at Acre, Odessa, Alexandria or Tientsin; and above all to remain a fleet-in-being of overwhelming superiority. The only interesting exception was Codrington's joint fleet action, with the French and Russians against the Turks at Navarino.

A century of inaction by capital ships had bred a widespread indifference to gunnery and imaginative tactics. What counted most at the beginning of the twentieth century was spit and polish. Wealthy captains paid from their own pockets for lavish but purely ornamental fittings that would have been more appropriate to a millionaire's yacht. Smartness was all. A yet more serious malady remained endemic: below flag rank senior officers were not meant to understand the strategy of war, or even possess the tactical expertise to manoeuvre a fleet. Admiral Lord Charles Beresford stated that

> 'he was now 56 years old, with one foot in the grave, and he had only handled three ships for five hours in his life, and that was a great deal more than some of his brother admirals.'

Suddenly on attaining flag rank, or even when finally in command of a fleet, a strategic and tactical genius was presumed to emerge, fully equipped. Nor did the Admiralty provide any effective school for such belated training.

A great lover of the Royal Navy, one of its most distinguished historians, has referred to it, having run in a rut for nearly a century, as 'a drowsy, inefficient, moth-eaten organisation'.

At the turn of the century came a development of vast significance: the Germans began to show unmistakeable signs of naval ambition. To have the most professional army in Europe was not enough. They wished to be second to none at sea. Formal German Navy Laws were introduced in 1898 and 1900 setting out their avowed target—a fleet so powerful that 'if the strongest naval power engaged it, it would endanger its own supremacy'. And this attitude was supported by hostile propaganda and stimulated by the Boer War.

But in Britain there was no certainty that Germany would in the event be the enemy. Russia was always a possible opponent, and the tragi-comedy in 1904 when the doomed Russian fleet—terrified of purely imaginary Japanese torpedo-boats—fired on some Hull trawlers, served to underline the dubious situation. Even the Anglo-French Entente was still in the mists of the future when Queen Victoria died, and the French rivalled the Germans in bitter hostility to Britain.

In 1901 Britain stood in perilous isolation. 'She was disliked by Germany, suspected by France, and looked upon by Russia as the eternal enemy.'[1] Ten years later Britain had joined France and Russia to form the Triple Entente. There should no longer be any suspicion that this was intended as an aggressive alliance. All three countries desired peace, if only for reasons of self-preservation.

Amid all these political gropings and later regroupings, the inventors were busy. Revolutionary advances in engineering, design, and weaponry were under way. One of the most sensational was seen first as a small piece of impudence at the 1897 Review. Suddenly, among the fifty vast, sluggish battleships there appeared a tiny craft, which drove, at a speed wholly outside all previous experience, down the lines of great ships. She was Charles Parsons' *Turbinia*, with 2,000 horsepower driving nine screws. Her actual speed reached the incredible nineteenth-century figure of 34 knots. (The fastest battleship in 1904 had a designed speed of 18.5 knots.) This brilliant demonstration soon led to an order for turbine-driven destroyers, and one of these, the *Viper*, attained in 1899 37 knots—a sensational and unprecedented speed.

As to gunnery there were at first two barriers to progress—the poor quality and design both of the guns and the control system; and the hostility of most captains and commanders to spoiling their gleaming paint and polished metal with the grimy accompaniments of firing practice. It was even known that in some cases the practice shells were thrown overboard, as a happy and advantageous alternative to firing them.

The attractive and important function of 'showing the flag' throughout the world had, almost imperceptibly, forced the harsh realities of battle practice into the background. And when gunnery exercises were carried out, the official ranges were controlled, and limited to 2,000 yards. This might have seemed to Nelson a scarcely perceptible advance on his own day.

Even more improbable was the fact that the Royal Navy

[1] Buchan, *The King's Grace*.

retained in 1900 a large number of muzzle-loading guns, almost the last navy to do so.

The towering figure of Admiral Sir John Fisher began to emerge unmistakeably on an epic scale in 1899, with his appointment as Commander-in-Chief of the Mediterranean Fleet. He was then aged fifty-eight. He had joined the Navy in 1854. He himself stemmed from relatively unprivileged stock; and he was later to launch regular attacks on the system whereby most naval officers were drawn from a restricted class.

'This democratic country won't stand 99 per cent *at least* of her Naval Officers being drawn from the "Upper Ten". It's amazing to me that anyone should persuade himself that an aristocratic Service can be maintained in a democratic state. The true democratic principle is Napoleon's: *"La carrière ouverte aux talents!".'*

In the year of the Diamond Jubilee the Royal Navy could muster among its officers two princes, two dukes, a viscount, a count, an earl and eight baronets. None of this was, *per se*, of the smallest moment; and Jackie Fisher was not so stupid as to be an inverted snob. But he was writing in 1902 :

'Brains, character, and manners are not the exclusive endowment of those whose parents can afford to spend £1,000 on their education . . . Let every fit boy have his chance, irrespective of the depth of his parents' purse.'

Fisher made a rough calculation that there were only 3 per cent of the population in a position to cope with this monetary barrier.

'The remainder of the population is 41,500,000 and of these no single one can ever hope to become an officer in the Navy! Surely we are drawing our Nelsons from too narrow a class.'[2]

Fisher's passionate devotion to the Service prompted a host of changes that for him were vital to the very existence of his country. As First Sea Lord (1904–10) he soon encountered a

[2] Marder, *Fear God and Dread Nought.*

4

multitude of hostile and influential opponents, and his letters to his friends demonstrate unconcealed fury at their obtuseness. Vitriolic, libellous, even unjust, they still stir our emotions. His genuine religious zeal had given him a detailed knowledge of the Bible, and his diatribes resound with an Old Testament fervour. His enemies were designated as traitors, whose 'wives should be widows, their children fatherless, their homes a dunghill'. And yet behind all this venom, and his special version of the three 'Rs'—'Ruthless, Relentless and Remorseless'—he was a kindly, almost naive, person, adored by children, who particularly loved his endearing way of letting them try on his admiral's coat blazing with stars.

Of all the naval 'Milestones to Armageddon', as Winston Churchill called one of his most famous chapters, the most significant was the birth in 1905 of HMS *Dreadnought*. Her genesis, and the related creation in 1906 of the *Invincible* class of battle cruiser—an entirely fresh concept in terms of speed and heavy guns—led directly to such major confrontations as occurred at sea in 1914–18. It also led, at least indirectly, to the *Goeben* episode. Perhaps the story of the *Dreadnought* is by now as familiar as it deserves to be. But it cannot be silently bypassed. The most striking feature was the speed with which she was designed, laid down, launched and completed within an unprecedented time limit. From the laying of her keel-plate to her going to sea for trials occupied a year and a day. One almost senses that the shadow of Fisher's celebrated 'dunghill' must have lain across the minds of those in charge, whether in or out of uniform!

One of the main features of HMS *Dreadnought*, the most original capital ship ever launched, was that she was the first turbine-engined big ship in any navy. Her speed of 21 knots made her 2 knots faster than any rival of similar size.

Again much of the *Goeben* story centres on gunnery, and the foundations of British naval gunnery were being laid at this same time. The *Dreadnought* was equipped with ten 12-inch guns, a great advance on all previous capital ships. By 1904 the

Kaiser had got wind of this intention through his highly efficient Naval Attaché in London. With the Krupp factories to back his able designers, it was clearly only a matter of time until Germany, given the chance, would herself take the lead in this important advance. There was one special problem, and it was specifically hers. The Kiel canal, which was essential to the rapid passage of warships between their North Sea bases and the Baltic, was too narrow and shallow for this modern class of battleship. So, once committed to this new project, the German High Seas Fleet would be greatly restricted till the major project of enlarging the canal was complete; this in turn would not be before the summer of 1914—a daunting delay. And this of course was clearly a bonus for Fisher. In Professor Marder's phrase, he had 'converted the Kiel Canal into a useless ditch'.

Meantime there were numerous gunnery developments: by 1910 Britain had completed seven ships with ten 12-inch guns, while Germany had only four ships with guns of rather smaller (11-inch) calibre; the German navy in fact had to wait until 1911 before equipping any of her ships with the 12-inch gun.

Unhappily all this dictatorial vigour made for Fisher bitter enemies, of whom the chief was Lord Charles Beresford. It is unnecessary to exhume this sad feud which threatened to tear the Navy in two. But to the lasting credit of both men, one judgement must be quoted. At the end of his professional life, Beresford wrote in his Memoirs: 'From a 12-knot Fleet with numerous breakdowns, [Fisher] made a 15-knot Fleet without breakdowns.' This was more than merely handsome—it was the plain truth.

Admiral Fremantle, who was to fulfil an important role in the drama of the *Goeben*, said of Fisher:

'His great claim to fame is that he succeeded in making us *think*. Before he asserted himself the spirit and discipline of the Navy were excellent, but we were in a groove in which merit was decided and rewards given for smartness in drills, in appearance, and in handling [ships] in close order. Fisher got us out of that groove and made us realize that the object of our existence was fighting, and that our training, our habits, our exercises, and our thoughts must always have that in view.'[3]

Fisher himself had his moments of unbalance. On two widely separated occasions, in 1904 and 1908, he suggested to King Edward, with whom he was on happy and admiring terms, that the Fleet might take a leaf out of Nelson's book and 'Copenhagen' the German Fleet at anchor, without warning—a kind of proleptic anticipation of Pearl Harbour. The King's response was, 'My God, Fisher, you must be mad!' (And in fact Nelson had done nothing of the sort in *his* Battle of Copenhagen—it was another admiral who there forced the surrender of the Danish fleet, during peace time, two years after Trafalgar.) All the same the King was convinced, or at least he satisfied Fisher of his conviction, that war with Germany was inevitable.

Such was the man who, though by no means unassisted by other men of drive and vision, swept the Navy into the twentieth century.

But behind all these competitive innovations hung an uncertain political backdrop. The German Anglophobia had reached special levels of enmity in 1900, partly due to their disapproval of the Boer war. This public hostility even spilled over into rude caricatures of the aged Queen Victoria; though she still remained for her grandson, the Kaiser, a respected and at times an adored matriarchal figure. But the Kaiser was now signing letters to his cousin the Tsar, 'Admiral of the Atlantic', which suggested a naval ambition that might become paranoid. In this context there were a series of invasion scares in England, and at least one memorable piece of fictional propaganda—Erskine Childers' *The Riddle of the Sands*, published in 1903.

The pre-war role of Winston Churchill, whose name will forever be linked with the Royal Navy, is less simple than might at first appear. In 1906 he was an improbable leader of the

[3] Fremantle, *My Naval Career.*

7

pacifists, 'economists' and social reformers who desired a 'little Navy', and were intent that the nation's money should not be squandered on naval rivalries. (The term 'economist' in this context does not mean students of the theories of Malthus or Keynes. It simply signified those Radicals and others who wished for naval and military economies.)

The crisis—personal as well as political—came in 1909 when the advocates of a big navy were aiming at six new *Dreadnoughts* in the year's programme. Churchill and his friends, including Lloyd George, wanted only four. Even a keen fellow-Liberal like Lord Esher thought that Churchill was adopting this stance to curry favour with the Radical wing of his party. The Tories adopted the slogan: 'We want eight and we won't wait'. As Churchill himself, in his frankest manner, wrote years later:

> 'The Admiralty had demanded six ships: the economists [including himself] offered four: and we finally compromised on eight... But although the Chancellor of the Exchequer and I were right in the narrow sense, we were absolutely wrong in relation to the deep tides of destiny.'[4]

But in 1911, with an unlikely focal point—Agadir in Morocco—a fresh outbreak of German naval aggression occurred. It is unnecessary to go into the details, except to explain that the idea of the Germans establishing a new Atlantic naval base in North-West Africa was alarming to nearly all Britons. Even Lloyd George, still regarded as a near-pacifist (he had been a so-called pro-Boer in 1900), gave voice to strangely bellicose opinions. He informed a Mansion House audience that

> 'if a situation were to be forced on us in which peace could only be preserved ... by allowing Britain to be treated, where her interests were vitally affected, as if she were of no account in the Cabinet of Nations, then I say emphatically that peace at that price would be a humiliation intolerable for a great country like ours to endure.'

[4] *The World Crisis.*

This Agadir crisis concerns us mainly as being the prime cause of the remarkable 'General Post' which produced a new First Lord. Lord Haldane, whose work at the War Office had been highly effective, gave Asquith an ultimatum: either the Admiralty must set its house in order (and for this purpose there could be no better new broom than himself—a widely shared view); or he would resign as War Secretary. The upshot was that Churchill was appointed, at the age of thirty-six, to be First Lord of the Admiralty. With this was coupled the fixed intention of providing the Admiralty with a proper War Staff on military lines. Haldane had to accept the Woolsack.

Thus came about two events of momentous significance—the appointment of Churchill, and the formation of a War Staff; but there was only a woefully short time in which to move into top gear, though at the time none could guess that fate would allot a mere thirty months.

The quality of some senior officers—including Admiral Milne who was to play, or abstain from playing, a key role in the story of the *Goeben*—was a topic on which many younger sailors of distinction held severe opinions. Bertram Ramsey, a future admiral of splendid gifts, who was in charge of Operation Neptune in 1944, wrote of his squadron admiral:

'He won't admit that a knowledge of war is the least necessary for any officers until they come to flag rank, but how they are to learn it then I don't know . . . the old school will not admit that any one junior to them can have any ideas at all.'

In certain cases this was the view held about subordinate flag officers by their Commander-in-Chief. A highly informed sailor, Stephen King-Hall (himself the son of a capable old-world admiral) wrote even more severely:

'There were a number of shockingly bad admirals afloat in 1914. They were pleasant, bluff old sea-dogs, with no scientific training; endowed with a certain amount of common sense, they had no conception of the practice and theory of strategy or tactics.'[5]

Yet it is probable that in 1914 the public as a whole regarded the Navy as at the summit of its power and prestige.

The splendid fighting quality of the captains and admirals whose names are most justly remembered with honour—Beatty, Tyrwhitt, Goodenough, Keyes, Chatfield, the brothers Kelly and (despite all belated criticisms) Jellicoe, to name but a few—must never be forgotten. The problem was that in 1914 there were also many mediocrities who must needs be recognized as such, and eliminated. And as Admiral Sir William James, a prominent figure in both World Wars, told Chatfield in 1938:

'We embarked on a full dress war after 100 years of peace and after a dynamic revolution in weapons. Only a superman could have handled these weapons without making any mistakes.'

Fisher, too, made mistakes—as all great innovators must. But one of the neatest epitaphs on his life's work was presented to him in the last year of his life. It came from the surgeon who had saved the King's life in 1902, Sir Frederick Treves. 'As a prophet you have advantages over Jeremiah. You have lived to see your prophecies come true. He, poor man, did not.'

Perhaps the most dramatic and exact of Fisher's prophecies appeared in a letter characteristically headed: *Secret. Please burn.* The place was Lucerne where he was on holiday, and the time late in November, 1911. He wrote:

'My only two visits to Winston were fruitful. I tell you (AND YOU ONLY!) the whole secret of the changes! To get Jellicoe Commander-in-Chief of the Home Fleet prior to 21 October, 1914, which is the date of the Battle of Armageddon.'

[5] *My Naval Life.*

Such staggering, intuitive accuracy, and other similar lightning flashes of inspiration, deserve the name of genius. This was the prepotent and volcanic leader, without whom (in Admiral Bacon's verdict) we might have lost the war.

Just four months before the date quoted (the anniversary of Trafalgar), a Bosnian student, Gavrilo Princip, fired two shots at Sarajevo that killed the heir to the Austrian throne and swiftly set Europe ablaze.

This swings our narrative back to the political alignments against which all these naval developments must be set.

By 1914 the main opposition to the Triple Entente, of Britain, France and Russia, in this perilous balance of power, was Germany—linked with the huge, sprawling, but ineffective, Austro-Hungarian dinosaur. These, with an uncertain Italy, made up the Triple Alliance, or Central Powers, as they came to be known. There were also two other vital factors : Russia had taken Serbia under her protective wing; and France was under strong obligations to defend the neutrality of Belgium.

Outwardly the omens in the summer of 1914 seemed reasonably favourable—apart from the imminence of civil war in Ireland. From the Cabinet downwards, attention was focused —not for the last time—on the muddy boundaries of Fermanagh and Tyrone. This was the potential arena. But, far off, and all but forgotten, there was a state of bitter animosity between Austria and her small neighbour, Serbia. The Austrian generals and some at least of their statesmen were awaiting an excuse, a sign from heaven (or elsewhere), for launching a punitive campaign. For this purpose they believed that they could count on at least moral support from their German cousins.

In similar fashion Serbia had high hopes of Russian aid if a crisis arose, even though the Russians had no wish to be dragged into another Balkan war.

But it was the relationship between England and France that mattered most, especially in respect of their navies. As far back as 1908 there had been preliminary naval 'conversations' in

London; but to maintain absolute secrecy, nothing was committed to writing. Much more advanced conversations were again held in 1912. These included the conception of almost the entire French fleet being in the Mediterranean, with the implicit assurance that England would assist in guarding the French Channel ports. After many deliberations, joint signal books were prepared; but in January, 1914, the First Sea Lord vetoed their immediate use.

A single item in the long official record of proposals and counter-proposals must be mentioned. By what now seems an ironic chance, there is an entry dated 23.7.12 : 'Mediterranean. The question of command should be considered . . . (signed) E. Troubridge, C.O.S.'

The Gadarene rush towards war that followed the shots at Sarajevo was delayed initially for nearly a month, while Austria compiled crushing terms for her ultimatum to Serbia. The Kaiser had been yacht-racing off Kiel when the news of the assassination was brought to him, and had returned briefly to Berlin. Then—omitting to attend the funeral of his brother-Emperor's heir—he had gone off for a cruise in Norwegian waters, finally hurrying home as the crisis escalated.

Impulsively he had already told the Austrians that they could count on Germany's support. This was a blank cheque, and intended as such. There was no one with the influence, or the courage, to restrain him—even from annotating a despatch from his ambassador in Vienna : 'Now or never'.

A report of the ultimatum reached Britain on Friday, 24 July. Churchill was present at a Cabinet meeting where their despondent thoughts on Ireland were interrupted by 'the quiet grave tones of Sir Edward Grey's voice reading a document which had just been brought to him from the Foreign Office'. Although the Foreign Secretary spent part of the week-end fishing on the Itchen—for the leisured peacetime routine was not easily broken —the following twelve days were crammed with frantic but ultimately futile efforts for peace. Serbia sent a prompt and largely abject reply to the Austrian demands. But it was not enough—nothing short of complete abnegation of sovereignty would have satisfied the men in Vienna. And within forty-five minutes of receiving the Serbian reply, the Austrian envoy had left Belgrade on his way to the frontier.

The splendid foresight of Churchill and his First Sea Lord, Prince Louis of Battenberg, in delaying the dispersal of the fleets and their crews after the test mobilization at Portland, is justly famous; but it lies outside the mainstream of this narrative. Similarly the move that took the fleet from Portland to its war station at Scapa Flow in the Orkneys is relevant chiefly as the final attempt to persuade Germany that Britain's reaction to the crisis was serious.

But one telegram does concern us. On 27 July the Commander-in-Chief, Mediterranean, received—as did all senior Naval Commanders—a special message from the First Lord :

> 'European political situation makes war between Triple Alliance and Triple Entente Powers by no means impossible. This is not the "warning telegram" but be prepared to shadow possible hostile men-of-war ... Measure is purely precautionary. The utmost secrecy is to be observed and no unnecessary person is to be informed.[6]

The Anglo-French naval dispositions were clarified at long last on 2 August when Grey was finally able to tell the French that, if the German fleet came through the Straits of Dover to attack French ports, the Royal Navy would go into action against the intruder.

As to numbers, Britain had in all thirty-one modern capital ships against Germany's eighteen; so her position of absolute superiority appeared assured, and at the crucial moment. In the Mediterranean the French were also in an enviable position. Ignoring the question of age, their ratio of heavy ships, *vis-à-vis* the Germans, was 12 to 1.

[6] Milne Papers.

The rest of 'the easy descent to Avernus' is too familiar to need recounting. While great ships trailed each other in the dazzling Mediterranean sunlight of 4 August, the final warning telegram was sent out from the Admiralty. And at midnight, Central European Time, the British ultimatum to Germany expired.

2

The Whitehall Machine

'The First Lord had too inflated a conception of his functions.' MARDER

E VERYONE has his own image of the Royal Navy in its heyday. And in 1914 many regarded the Navy of that date as at the summit of its power and prestige. In face of a huge preponderance of ships, such opinions were hardly surprising. What was overlooked was the strange circumstance that this vast fleet had not fought a major action since 1815, when the war of 1812 came to a protracted finish.

Faced with this state of inanition, Haldane insisted (as we have seen) as the price of continuing as War Minister, that there should be a proper Naval War Staff. But McKenna, a colourless First Lord, shared with Fisher and his successor as First Sea Lord, Admiral Sir Arthur Wilson, a strong reluctance for any such body.

Churchill, on appointment to the Admiralty, could not risk recalling Fisher—he was too old at seventy for a peacetime post. Yet Admiral Wilson, the First Sea Lord, would himself be seventy in a few months, and due to retire then. So, fond as Churchill was of this elderly hero of the Sudan wars—in which, ashore, he had won a spectacular V.C.—it was agreed that Wilson must go. A dull replacement, Admiral Bridgeman, was the best that Churchill could contrive, and after a year the First Lord was busy getting rid of him—not without an embarrassing struggle—on the dubious grounds of alleged ill-health. Finally an effective First Sea Lord was installed. Prince Louis of Battenberg's sole disability was his German birth, being the eldest son of Prince Alexander of Hesse. Once, when reproached by an officious German admiral for not having joined the German Navy, he produced the splendid retort: 'Sir, when I joined the Royal Navy in the year 1868, the German Empire did not exist'. He had become a naturalized British subject and had married Princess Victoria, a granddaughter of Queen Victoria. His many talents commended him, and his genial and commanding personality confirmed him, as the beau-ideal of a senior admiral. His son became Admiral of the Fleet Earl Mountbatten of Burma.

With war only two years away, an Admiralty War Staff was at long last brought to birth. Outside the Navy almost everyone of consequence was pleased and even Fisher was in the end delighted. Churchill was congratulated 'most warmly upon the most pregnant reform which had been carried out by the Admiralty since the days of Lord St. Vincent'—who had died in 1823.

But the creation of a Staff did not automatically produce trained staff officers. Progress was slow, and in Admiral Dewar's pungent phrase, 'We had the opportunity but not the intellectual capital to float a staff.' He wrote:

'The efficiency of a staff can be judged by its orders and signals, and many of these emanating from the Admiralty were badly drafted, went into unnecessary details and indicated a general lack of supervision. It has been stated that on one occasion during August, when strict wireless silence had been ordered so as to conceal certain movements in the Heligoland Bight, the Admiralty commenced calling up one of the cruisers engaged in the operations. She refused to answer, but the calls continued hour after hour and thinking it might be important, eventually did so. The message then came through: "Has Herbert Brown, A.B., been discharged to hospital and did he take his kit with him?".'[1]

[1] *The Navy from Within.*

Battenberg himself did not wish to act as Chief of Staff; so there had to be a separate admiral holding this post, which inevitably carried little executive authority. One of Battenberg's officers wrote: 'He says he could not lower the position of his office by becoming the Chief of Staff to a civilian First Lord.'

The first officer to be appointed Chief of Staff was the man who was to hold the centre of the stage in the story of the *Goeben* —Rear-Admiral Ernest Troubridge. He held sufficient authority to draft the crucial memorandum in June, 1912, defining Admiralty policy in the Mediterranean. But his personal history can best be explored later.

It was natural, in the easy rhythm of peacetime, for the naval machine to be a trifle rusty—at least in Whitehall. Churchill recognized the insuperable difficulties.

'Our first labour was the creation of the War Staff ... But such a task requires a generation. No wave of the wand can create those habits of mind in Seniors on which the efficiency or even the reality of a Staff depends ... The dead weight of professional opinion was adverse. They had got on well enough without it before ... The Royal Navy had made no important contribution to Naval Literature. The standard work on Sea Power was written by an American Admiral.'

(The standard work today on the Navy of 1914–18 is also by an American historian.) To quote again from the First Lord's account written some years after the War:

'At the outset of the conflict we had more captains of ships than captains of war ... At least fifteen years of consistent policy were required to give the Royal Navy that widely extended outlook upon war problems and of war situations without which seamanship, gunnery, instrumentalisms of every kind, devotion of the highest order, could not achieve their due reward. Fifteen years! And we were only to have thirty months!'[2]

[2] *The World Crisis.*

It is essential to examine the nature and talents of the young man—he was thirty-six when first appointed—who as First Lord held sway over the whole vast organization. It is almost impossible to find anything original to say of the complex genius that Winston Churchill already presented. But two issues are vital to our understanding : the incomparable saviour of his country in 1940 must be distinguished from the assertive and combative First Lord, who in 1911 was relatively a youngster. Earlier, while at the Home Office, he had adopted a quasi-pacifist position and opposed the new naval expansion and the multiplication of Dreadnought battleships.

In this context it is relevant to look several years ahead to 1925. During his five lean years as Chancellor, Churchill laboured day and night, sustained by his own device of the 'Ten Years Rule', to obstruct Admiral Beatty's ambitious but reasonable cruiser programme. A sharp conflict was soon openly declared, and Beatty's letters disclose his anger and hostility.

'That extraordinary fellow Winston had gone mad. Economically mad, and no sacrifice is too great to achieve what in his shortsightedness is the panacea for all evils—to take a shilling off the Income Tax.'

Following his father's lead, Churchill's zest for economy as Chancellor (as indeed when he was Home Secretary) was almost as passionate as his drive for expansion when at the Admiralty.

Secondly, once in office, Churchill was determined to take on detailed responsibilities for which there were no precedents—at least for a civilian First Lord.

'I accepted full responsibility for bringing about successful results, and in that spirit I exercised a close general supervision over everything that was done or proposed. Further, I claimed and exercised an unlimited power of suggestion and initiative over the whole field, subject only to the approval and agreement of the First Sea Lord on all operative orders.'

With a touch of defiance he added : 'Right or wrong, that is what I did, and it is on that basis that I wish to be judged.' It is easy now to read between the lines and see how readily an aggressive civilian could over-rule an unassertive First Sea Lord. And perhaps Battenberg was too great a gentleman to fight fiercely for his own rights. At least one shrewd critic, Admiral Colville, who was far from ungenerous, said bleakly: 'It is pretty self-evident that (Battenberg) had become a nonentity and simple tool in Winston Churchill's hand.'

Churchill's zeal was not confined to the boardroom, but was noted also at sea. Asquith was amused at his antics when both were witnessing some gunnery practice. Churchill was seen dancing about behind the guns, elevating, depressing and sighting. The Prime Minister commented: 'My young friend yonder thinks himself Othello and blacks himself all over to play the part.'

Later he entered so fully into the role of supreme arbiter, if not dictator, as to make a habit of personally drafting operational signals. This was open to two serious objections: firstly rather more is required to produce a precise draft (whose meaning will be unambiguous) than a mastery of the English language. We shall shortly see how this very difficulty led to total confusion in a specific case. The second disadvantage was the stultifying effect that such dominance, by one who saw 'his business everything and his intent everywhere', was bound to have on the Sea Lords. To quote Marder's restrained verdict on a leader he greatly admired—'The First Lord had too inflated a conception of his functions'.

As war drew near, his commitment grew to be total. He recognized the nature of his own temperament, and during the last days of peace he wrote to his wife with wonderful insight and candour:

'I am interested, geared up and happy. Is it not horrible to be built like that? The preparations have a hideous fascination for me. I pray God to forgive me for such fearful levity.'

This apparent lust for war has been alleged by his enemies over many decades; but one fact must be recognized. Although not the most sensitive of men (except, naturally, where his own affairs were concerned), he had good reason to be keenly aware of the naked horrors of death and mutilation on the field of battle. He has left one of the classic accounts of an Advanced Dressing Station in May, 1915. This grim passage ends: '. . . the terrible spectacle of a man being trepanned. Everywhere was blood and bloody rags.' But this occurred in the last month of his time as head of the Navy. Many years earlier at the impressionable age of twenty-three he had seen, at the closest quarters, that war (in General Sherman's words) is hell. After the relatively easy success of the famous cavalry charge at Omdurman, he noted the price:

'There came a succession of grisly apparitions; horses spouting blood, struggling on three legs, men staggering on foot, men bleeding from terrible wounds, fish-hook spears stuck right through them, arms and faces cut to pieces, bowels protruding, men gasping, crying, collapsing, expiring. Our first task was to succour these.'[3]

No one knew better the daunting realities of battle, and assuredly his self-confessed, occasional 'levity' was not founded on ignorance.

Even as late as 1915, Asquith, who was at heart a warm supporter of his First Lord, wrote regretfully:

'It is a pity that Winston hasn't a better sense of proportion, and also a larger endowment of the instinct of loyalty . . . I am rarely fondly of him, but I regard his future with many misgivings . . . He will never get to the top in English politics, with all his wonderful gifts; to speak with the tongue of men and angels, and to spend laborious days and nights in administration, is no good if a man does not inspire trust.'[4]

We may smile at the infinite distance of Asquith's judgement from the fulfilment of 1940, but the passage serves to show the

[3] *My Early Life.*
[4] Roy Jenkins: *Asquith.*

• •

nature of the wide-spread distrust then felt towards this dazzling young man by those in high places—and elsewhere.

To glance briefly at the other members of the War Staff: Prince Louis was a seaman held in great respect, and few challenged his appointment as First Sea Lord at the end of 1912. Later his health was a source of worry; but it seems likely that he foresaw—as indeed happened—that he would be the victim of hostile prejudice on account of his German blood, if war came with Germany. And when the *Goeben* crisis developed, the clouds of innuendo were already gathering around him, aggravated by a monstrous press campaign.

The Second Sea Lord was Admiral Hamilton, not a distinguished officer, who was shortly dropped. The Chief of Staff was Admiral Sturdee who, before the year 1914 ended, was to win the only overwhelming British naval victory of the war—the Battle of the Falkland Islands. The baronetcy which he thus earned, by tradition, for a major victory at sea was the first to be conferred since 1811. But at this stage he was responsible for the War Staff; and under him, as one authority has put it, the Staff slumbered. Adverse comments by contemporaries on his inadequacy and his resistance to advice—let alone criticism—abound.

'Sturdee has been one of the curses to the Navy [as Chief of Staff]. He was principally responsible for all our disasters afloat, and Fisher showed his acumen by turning him out,'

wrote Beatty to his wife in November, 1914. Admiral Oliver, the Naval Secretary (who achieved the rare distinction of reaching his century), wrote of him as 'a pompous man who would never listen to anyone else's opinion. I could not stick him'. And the brilliant and pungent Admiral Richmond commented:

'Everything was impossible to this absurd amateur historian of a Chief of Staff. If we lose the best part of our fleet he will have a heavy charge to answer—he and the Sea Lords ... His attitude of incompetence and impotence makes me furious.'

'Fatuous and self-satisfied'. 'It is quite extraordinary to observe the nausea which any proposal for offensive action induces in the Chief of Staff . . .'

and so on for many more diary entries.[5] When every allowance is made for Richmond's personal resentment, it is a grim indictment. Marder's careful judgement on Sturdee is more balanced and hence more valid.

'His trouble was that he thought he was the only man who knew anything about war . . . He lacked the gift of leadership and never used the brains of his subordinates.'

The Secretary to this curious team was Sir William Graham Green, uncle to his more famous namesake, a man respected for his wisdom, energy and dependability—'a tower of strength to all departments'. Every morning these five men met—'the supreme and isolated centre of naval war direction', as Churchill put it.

The general poor esteem which this War Staff inspired is sad to record. Even an official (and originally classified) Naval Staff Mongraph stated in 1929 that

'with the exception of the six [officers] from the War College, it may be doubted whether any of the officers who were summoned hastily to recruit the War Staff had ever made a special study of any aspect of naval war. Nor were they conversant with the procedure of Admiralty business.'

'We are', wrote Richmond, then Assistant Director of Naval Operations, after six weeks of war, 'the most appalling amateurs who ever tried to conduct a war.' And later he added :

'A "Staff" was established a few years ago with the sounding title of "War Staff". There is the gravest reason for suspicion that the so-called Staff was not in reality a Staff at all . . . The British Public has believed, no doubt, that the War Staff was

[5] Marder, *Portrait of an Admiral*.

employed upon the preparation for war . . . One imagines the Staff studying the naval problems in home and foreign waters, the influence of this or that new weapon, its probable employment by the enemy, its most proper employment by ourselves. These would, it is feared, be idle imaginings.'[6]

As regards a limited approach to planning a single example at the highest level will serve. On 5 August, the day after Britain entered the war, Churchill met Richmond and said, 'Now we have our war. The next thing is to decide how we are going to carry it on.' Richmond admits that he was severely shaken by this 'damning confession'.

A thirty-two-year-old commander, later Admiral Thursfield, who served in the Operations Division in 1914, commented:

'Neither the Chief of the War Staff nor the Director of Operations Division seemed to have any particular idea of what the War Staff was supposed to be doing, or how they should make use of it.'

To quote again from the Naval Staff Monograph on this subject: 'The War Staff had been working for barely two years when war broke out . . . It proved unable to cope with its tremendous task.' And finally to give an opinion by Admiral Lord Beatty: in 1925 he spoke of disasters that were 'the direct result of the lack of a sufficient and efficient Staff . . . We paid very dearly for the experience which led to its formation.'

It need hardly be added that, as the months of testing passed, the achievements of the Admiralty developed magnificently—notably the masterly task of defeating the U-boats, and the triumphs of the Intelligence Division under Captain (later Admiral Sir Reginald) Hall and his superlative team of cryptographers. But our concern is with the leadership up to September, 1914, and the deficiencies of a mchine that was inevitably beset by teething troubles. How these affected the *Goeben*'s 'flight' we shall see.

[6] *Portrait of an Admiral.*

3

Two Contrasting Admirals

'An illustrious name, worthily sustained.'

ASQUITH TO TROUBRIDGE

BOTH the British admirals who were to be so closely associated with the *Goeben* had unusual backgrounds.

Admiral Sir Archibald Berkeley Milne, known in the Service
as 'Arky Barky', came from a family strongly linked with the
Navy. His grandfather was an admiral, while his father rose to a
lofty, though peacetime, position as an Admiral of the Fleet and
was created a baronet. In 1855 the son was born into a suitable
setting—his father's official residence at the Admiralty. With so
privileged a background he could naturally expect, in those days,
to serve mainly in flagships under a succession of naval celebri-
ties, and so it turned out. But at the age of twenty-seven he embarked on what even his highly uncritical obituarist called 'a
different career as a sea courtier'. In fact he spent almost half
of the next eighteen years in royal yachts. There were still dizzier
heights to come, for in 1903 he was appointed rear-admiral in
charge of HM yachts. In the conventional phrase 'he rapidly won
the affection and regard of the Prince and Princess of Wales'—
and we know that this debonair bachelor remained a particular
friend of Queen Alexandra's. The charge by a major historian
that he owed his rapid promotion to Court influence would seem
well founded, and as early as 1911 Fisher was writing to one of
the many ladies who received his platonic confidences:

'My dear sweet Jane... The greatest triumph of all [in a series of recent important promotions] is getting Jellicoe Second-in-Command of the Home Fleet... Sir Berkeley Milne, a serpent of the lowest type, thought he was sure [of that job]; he went to Balmoral and crawled. He... got knocked out.'

His hobbies were varied, and beyond the country gentleman's usual accomplishments as fisherman and deer-stalker, he collected rare orchids.

Milne's appearance was dapper to a degree. It was not unknown for flag officers to adapt their service dress to their personal whims within limits—Beatty is the obvious example. Milne affected a stiff turn-down collar with a black bow tie. This made a striking contrast with his white well-trimmed beard and his heavy black moustache. Perhaps he gave to some an impression of vanity, an air of effortless superiority that was to prove ill-founded.

Externals aside, it is not easy to form an accurate estimate of his professional worth as a seaman or tactician. But we get a glimpse of his quality from an entry in Admiral Richmond's diary for 1909. During an exercise Milne had passed a signal from his Commander-in-Chief by flags from ship to ship down the line. Admiral May asked him 'Why he had not hauled out of the line and fired a gun and made a signal by searchlight. "I should never think of doing that," said Milne. He meant that it was an improper thing to do... but equally it meant that he never *would* have thought of it, and there is the condemnation of Milne.'[1]

In peacetime the quadrille-like movements of squadrons did not inspire or demand much originality. As a second-in-command Milne served under three senior admirals, the last of whom was Fisher's arch-enemy, Lord Charles Beresford. This did nothing to soften Fisher's response to Milne's appointment by Churchill to be Commander-in-Chief Mediterranean in April, 1912. At this

[1] *Portrait of an Admiral.*

point a storm broke over the First Lord's head. Fisher, for the moment unemployed (he was seventy-two), wrote to answer Churchill's admission that he had 'provided for Milne . . . adequately, but not inordinately'—and his anger and contempt knew no bounds.

'I fear this must be my last communication with you in any matter at all. I am sorry for it, but I consider you have betrayed the Navy . . . and what the pressure could have been to induce you to betray your trust is beyond my comprehension. *You are aware that Sir Berkeley Milne is unfitted to be the Senior Admiral afloat, as you have now made him . . . I can't believe that you foresee all the consequences!* The results would be IRREPARABLE, IRREMEDIABLE, ETERNAL!'[2]

To Troubridge, now Chief of the War Staff, Fisher wrote from Naples:

'I've sent Winston back a letter to say I don't want to have any more correspondence with him, AS I JUST CAN'T HAVE ANYTHING TO DO WITH ANYONE WHO TRUCKLES! I HAVE GOT FROM OTHER RELIABLE QUARTERS WHAT WENT ON and I can only say to you in complete confidence that the whole lot of them will *all* be d—d well sold!!! Believe me my beloved Troubridge that it NEVER pays to do the wrong thing! The late King (God bless him!) used to tell me I was "d—d obstinate". I invariably replied "Forgive me your Majesty, *only firm!*".'[3]

In the same week as this explosion, Fisher was writing to Esher:

'Winston, alas! (as I have had to tell him) feared for his wife the social ostracism of the Court and succumbed to (Milne's) appointment—*a wicked wrong . . . The mischief is done!* Milne, an utterly useless Commander (Asquith leaned across

[2] Marder, *Fear God and Dread Nought.*
[3] Troubridge Papers.

McKenna on the Front Bench and said so to Winston), is now the senior Admiral afloat.'

Finally the vials of Fisher's wrath spilled over to include Battenberg. 'I told Winston that he was only a superior sort of *commis voyageur,* but *quite excellent at details* of organization.'[4] It would, of course, be absurd to take all Fisher's letters (often endorsed 'PLEASE BURN' or, in this case, 'Please don't mention the contents of this letter to a living soul') at their face value. But Fisher, for all his verbal excesses, was often a shrewd interpreter of current naval attitudes. His vitriolic outpourings certainly make clear to later generations how much bitterness had crept in to disrupt what Churchill himself has called 'the "Band of Brothers" tradition which Nelson had handed down', and which was now temporarily discarded.

Apart from suggestions of possible Court influence, it is natural to question Churchill's motives in offering Milne this appointment. The First Lord, it is now well known, was far from receptive to any interference by the King; they had had very sharp words on the not very vital subject of the names for new ships. (King George was not amused at the idea of a warship being named *Oliver Cromwell,* and one can see his point.) At this early stage of his time as First Lord, his Naval Secretary was David Beatty; and it is hard to think that this dashing officer, who had a big say in senior appointments, would have been keen to see Milne promoted to such influential heights.

As to the earlier relationship between Milne and Troubridge, we know only that their paths crossed through service in the Royal Yacht. And it is perhaps significant that Troubridge preserved only one letter from Milne, and this in the context of the Yacht. Milne wrote to recommend Sub-Lieutenant K. for service in the *Victoria and Albert* in these terms : 'a thorough gentleman, clean, well-dressed, good manners and an excellent officer.' This reinforces one's impression that Milne was apt to confuse service priorities.

[4] *Fear God and Dread Nought.*

In 1914 this undisputed charmer of royal ladies was faced with the more exacting demands of war. It is hardly surprising that he was swiftly weighed in the balances—and found wanting.

It is a relief to turn to an incomparably more attractive character, Rear-Admiral Ernest Troubridge. This genial sailor, generous in build and mind, could look back with excusable pride at a splendid line of ancestors, who had proved themselves as fighting men of the utmost gallantry.

Since the crisis, so soon to come, was to leave an impression, even in naval circles, of a reluctant admiral, we must look back some distance to establish Troubridge's antecedents; for in such a case they can hardly fail to influence our view of the man himself.

His great-grandfather was Rear-Admiral Sir Thomas Troubridge the first baronet, who was Nelson's close friend and described by him as 'the most meritorious sea officer of his standing in the service'; and by Admiral Lord St Vincent as having 'honour and courage bright as his sword'. He had the misfortune, while pressing on to reach his station for the battle of the Nile, to run his ship aground. Later authorities might have had him court-martialled, but Nelson's generous response was to express a 'very strong wish' that he be given the gold medal for the battle. Nine years later he was lost when his flagship foundered without trace. The next Troubridge, Sir Edward, fought at Copenhagen (1801) and was later a rear-admiral. His son, a colonel in the Crimea, lost his right leg and left foot at Inkerman. Lord Raglan, in his despatch, mentioned that, 'though desperately wounded he behaved with the utmost gallantry and composure'. (These were not idle words from one who had borne in silence the amputation of an arm at Waterloo.)

Admiral Sir Ernest Troubridge preserved among his papers a letter from a certain Hugh McLoughlin who had served as a corporal with Colonel Sir Thomas Troubridge in the Crimea, and who wrote to his son of having witnessed 'his noble courage, chivalrous devotion made under the greatest difficulty, in what must be his agony and pain, shattered and bleeding, his wounds exposed to a piercing frosty wind—no bandages ... This valiant soldier who I am certain gave credit to every man under his command, none to himself.'[5]

Sir Thomas Troubridge's third son is the man whose story concerns us. He was born in 1862—seven years after Milne—and followed the usual career of a young officer. He attracted special notice in 1888, when he saved the life of a young signal-man who fell overboard, in the darkness, from a torpedo boat going at full speed. This earned him the silver medal of the Royal Humane Society—and rightly put him in that fortunate category of men, whether sailors, soldiers, or civilians, whose courage is widely recognized as beyond dispute.

His family connections gave him an easy entrée, as a young lieutenant, into Edwardian Society. Few doors were closed to him, certainly not those of either 10 Downing Street or of York Cottage, Sandringham—the unpretentious home of Prince George (later George V). Such opportunities, in Troubridge's case, had nothing to do with social climbing; but they gave him the ear of men like Fisher and Asquith and the Prince of Wales, who were prepared to listen to the views of a highly intelligent and progressive young naval officer, and to use him on occasion to propagate, with discretion, their own opinions.

He was on agreeable terms with Prince George, who was three years his junior, and who, until the death of his elder brother in 1892, had followed a normal naval career up to the rank of commander. Of his letters which Troubridge kept, the first is an acknowledgement of condolences on his brother's death, through which he came into direct line with the throne. Three years later the Prince was writing after the birth of his second son, Albert (later George VI): 'No doubt he will join the Navy, the profession that we both love so well.'

Britain was well represented during the Russo-Japanese war

5 Troubridge Papers.

of 1904 with observers of the calibre of General Sir Ian Hamilton; Captain Troubridge as Naval Attaché at Tokyo was the only non-combatant European officer to witness some of the naval actions. His reports made a very favourable impression in Whitehall, and he received a number of decorations. One of these, the MVO, was described as 'a mark of his Majesty's personal appreciation'. Later he was Flag Captain in the battleship *Queen*. He was also to acquire a further reputation not merely as a tough seaman, but as a staff officer. The First Lord, Reginald McKenna, appointed him as his Naval Secretary, a post later to be held by Beatty under Churchill. Then, with the formation of the Naval War Staff, Troubridge was promoted to be the first Chief of Staff. Already he had enjoyed an unusually varied apprenticeship.

Some happy phrases from Fisher's highly coloured correspondence are worth preserving:

'I can't sufficiently thank you for your delightful letter! I much value it and its comfort! The ring of right in it!' '. . . a man of your calibre'. 'I had the pleasure of meeting Mrs Troubridge in the Abbey and lost my heart!'[6] *The Times* has some secret information about Turkey which is of importance . . . Yours till the angels smile on us. F.'[7]

His appointment as Chief of War Staff in 1912 drew an especially warm response from Sir Julian Corbett, then the doyen of naval historians:

'It is a real satisfaction to me that the "Staff" is to start under your auspices, for I know it requires powers which are perhaps the rarest among the good qualities I have learned to appreciate in the Navy. It is a fine thing to have the handling and fitting of such a machine and above all the confidence for the work, which your deep study and wide experience must have given you.

'I hope to see you set it on its way to fill the only serious gap

[6] Radclyffe Hall later lost her heart to the same lady.
[7] Troubridge Papers.

that remains, and I fear it will be uphill work till the new generation of trained officers arises to assist you.'

One of Troubridge's finest achievements in his positions of increasing influence was to keep clear of the prolonged and bitter feud between Fisher and Beresford—both egged on by their supporters. The day following a Trafalgar speech by 'Charlie B.' in 1909 the Admiral found he had omitted the honoured name of Troubridge from his list of notables, and he hastened to send his disarming amends: Beresford acclaimed ... 'the brilliant career of your great ancestor ... [and] the respect and esteem in which you yourself are held by all your brother officers'.

And to head the wave of approval for his key Admiralty appointment in 1912, the Prime Minister wrote in his own hand (as was regarded by many in high places as common courtesy in those more leisured days):

'My dear Admiral,

   Will you allow me to offer you most hearty congratulations on your new appointment.

   On personal grounds, it gives me great pleasure in recollection of happy days and scenes, which we have shared.

   But, apart from this, it is a great satisfaction that an illustrious name, worthily sustained, should be associated with a fresh and (as I confidently believe) most fruitful development of Admiralty administration.

Yours sincerely
H. H. Asquith.'[8]

Part of this growing reputation was due to Troubridge's readiness to speak his mind frankly, when so invited, even to very senior officers. As far back as 1906 Fisher's secretary and 'devil', Captain Crease, received (in modern terms) a 'rocket' from Troubridge for soliciting an opinion, for Fisher's use but in Crease's name. At once, the latter wrote back to say, 'Sir John desires me to state that he knows, of course, that you will give him your opinion whether you agree with him or not, and that

[8] Troubridge Papers.

is what he wants, and is why he is addressing himself to you.'
At this date Troubridge was only half way up the captains' list.

In November, 1912, Troubridge received a letter in the First
Lord's own fluent handwriting :

'My dear Troubridge,

Your position on the list makes it impossible for me to offer
you the position of 2nd in Command in the Mediterranean;
but I am vy glad to be able to offer you the command of
the Mediterranean cruisers. The *Defence* wh is returning
from China to exchange with the *Hampshire* will be available
for your Flagship . . .

Yours sincerely

Winston S. Churchill.'[9]

In this fashion, after three years at the Admiralty, he was
appointed as Rear-Admiral Commanding the cruiser squadron
in the Mediterranean, and by 1914 he was second-in-command
to Milne. The ill-fated partnership was under way.

One notes, even in a photograph, Troubridge's handsome
face, the fine head, the rugged profile, the genial lines around
the eyes. The whole effect conveys a welcoming air of solid
worth, absolute trustworthiness, and rock-like loyalty. It is easy
to see why he was held in high esteem and affection by his men,
who in deference to his thick, white hair nicknamed him 'The
Silver King'. It would not be possible to envisage an officer less
likely to be tried by Court Martial on a charge of 'forbearing to
pursue . . an enemy'—from negligence.

With so proud and impressive a heritage, it followed that the
old-fashioned concept of 'honour' was to him no empty phrase.
And the anguished cry to his Flag Captain at the crisis of his
career—'Think of my pride'—was for such a man neither empty
nor vain. It represented all that he held most precious. His
family tradition had long been summed up in their motto :

'Ne Cede Arduis'—Yield to no difficulties.

[9] Troubridge Papers.

4

The Turkish Labyrinth

'Scandalous, crumbling, decrepit, penniless Turkey.'

CHURCHILL

IN 1914 politicians found it difficult, even impossible, to make an accurate assessment of Turkey, her intentions or her potential.

The Sublime Porte,[1] the quaint name commonly used for the Turkish Government was, like a later Russia, 'a riddle wrapped in a mystery inside an enigma'. The title, which dated back to the early seventeenth century, had once carried an aura of mystery and authority. But Western observers later adopted a much more jaundiced view, and spoke contemptuously of 'the sick man of Europe'.

As far back as 1911, when in danger from Italy, Turkey had made an overture for an alliance with Britain. This was spurned, though even so bellicose a minister as Churchill was a trifle apprehensive at the foreseeable consequences. He wrote an unusually woolly note to the Permanent Under-Secrtary at the Foreign Office, Sir Arthur Nicolson:

'Will it not if it comes to war or warlike tension throw Turkey into Germany's arms more than ever?... Do you think it possible that Germany has been marking time for this to happen in order to secure an atmosphere more suited to

---

[1] A nickname, the 'high gate', for the centre of Government.

thunderbolts? . . . Clearly we must prefer Italy to Turkey *on all grounds—moral and unmoral*.'[2]

One influential supporter of the Ottoman Empire was Kaiser Wilhelm II, who took some trouble (and made some trouble) in cultivating the Turks. He even paid two visits at the end of the century to Turkey, and made some pro-Islamic speeches in his flamboyant manner. Germany sought a peaceful penetration of the Sultan's lands, and started work on a project to drive a railway to Baghdad.

The bad relationship between Germany and the members of the Entente (Britain, France and Russia) was not helped by the rivalries of the 'great' powers in their economic domination of Turkey. Germany continued to invest heavily in trade and armaments during the thirty years that led up to the war. Britain led the field in both imports and exports, and the French shared with Britain a specific and influential monopoly through the Banque Impériale Ottomane, a joint Anglo-French enterprise.

In the military field the 'sick man' needed a lot of aid. By 1914 the patient was under the care of two specialist physicians —a German Military Mission, and a British Naval Mission. The former was headed by General Liman von Sanders, a name that grew to be feared with good reason during the Gallipoli campaign. Von Sanders was a competent fighting soldier, though at first he showed little sign of sharing his Emperor's enthusiasm for his semi-political task. However, his work soon bore fruit. One British expert, Sir Edwin Pears, noted the considerable increase of German officers.

'I found Turkish soldiers everywhere being carefully and thoroughly drilled. The discipline was evidently stricter, and the officers in particular left the impression that they expected soon to be called upon to march.'

In 1913, when his summons came, von Sanders was commanding a division at Cassel. Later that year he was called to hear from the All-Highest what the scope of his job was to be.

[2] *The World Crisis.*

'It must be entirely immaterial to you whether the Young Turks are in power or the Old Turks. You are concerned with the army alone. In Constantinople you will meet Admiral Limpus, head of the British Naval Mission. Maintain good relations with each other. He works for the navy, you for the army. Each has his separate sphere.'[3]

The Young Turks—called in Turkish 'Ittihad ve Terakki' (the Union and Progress party)—were a growing force, brilliantly led by Enver Pasha who was to play a crucial part in this story.

The British Naval Mission was of much longer standing—it had been introduced in 1908, and four years later Rear-Admiral Arthur Limpus, essentially a staff officer, was appointed as its head. Both Missions were of impressive size, with a staff of about seventy. Limpus and his predecessors had an uphill task. In 1903, Lord Selborne, the First Lord of the Admiralty, had rated the Turkish navy as 'non-existent, absolutely and without qualification'. At that time her only gunboat capable of getting up steam in an emergency was in fact devoid of both coal and provisions. The Director of Naval Intelligence was safe in saying that the Turkish navy was 'quite useless for fighting'. In 1912, during the war with Italy they proved the justice of this opinion.

Stimulated by our Naval Mission, the Turks did a little better at sea during the Balkan Wars of 1912–13. Limpus was notion-ally Naval Adviser to the Ottoman Ministry of Marine, yet remained a flag officer on the active list of the Royal Navy. It was noted that he found his task such a strain that he took refuge in heavy cigar-smoking, an exercise he pursued even in his bath. Probably his chief contribution was to obtain valuable contracts for the building of warships in British yards. In 1911 two Dread-noughts were ordered from Armstrong and Vickers; these were of the latest kind, of 23,000 and 28,000 tons, and with ten 13.5-inch guns and fourteen 12-inch guns respectively. They were due for completion towards the autumn of 1914. Limpus had been keen a year earlier on an immediate sale of two pre-Dreadnought

[3] *Five Years.*

battleships for a price around £150,000, but the project, though backed by Churchill as First Lord, did not get under way.

The relations between Churchill and his representative in Turkey were not altogether cloudless. Randolph Churchill has revealed the slightly comic situation in 1913. Admiral Limpus favoured an unconventionally informal tone for his demi-official letters to the First Lord. One of these read:

'If it interests you, you shall have the whole yarn when I return; just now there is no need to trouble you with more than the first two pages of the first letter [giving details of local progress] ... The Turks have built the *Rechadieh*.[4] They need a dock for her. Their arsenals in the Golden Horn are crumbling—have nearly crumbled to decay. They need capable management, workmen, and money. [Limpus then set out the terms of the proposed Anglo-Turkish naval agreement.] Of course the unforeseen is always to be reckoned with, but barring the unforeseen a really useful work has been born. Its nationality is very distinctly British, and if I do not mistake, undesirable aliens are shut out for 30 years. If that is so, then quite apart from the other odds and ends of work that have to be done, we have justified our mission both to the Turks and to those who sent us.

'It is bad to shout too soon, but the appearance of the infant is so healthy that the temptation to cheer a little is strong.'

This chirpy and constructive letter may not be a literary gem, but the First Lord was affronted, and loud in condemnation of its form. Accordingly the fifty-one-year-old admiral was given a brisk lecture on style:

'I find it necessary to criticize the general style and presentment of your letters. A flag officer writing to a member of the Board of Admiralty on service matters ought to observe a

---

[4] This ship and her various names are a potential trap for the unwary. Starting as the *Sultan Mehmet Rechad V*, she was renamed the *Rashadieh*, or *Rechadieh*—modernized as *Reshadiye*. Later she served in the Royal Navy as the *Erin*.

36

proper seriousness and formality. The letters should be well written or typed on good paper; the sentences should be complete and follow the regular form,'

and so on at some length.[5] This type of 'somewhat unkindly' assault (as the writer's son concedes) does a lot to explain why the youthful First Lord steadily collected a fair quota of enemies from among his senior naval advisers.

Germany had few illusions about Turkey's potential. Even in mid-1814, von Moltke, the Chief of Staff in Berlin, did not look on Turkey as an asset, and the German military authorities reserved the right to bring home their entire Mission if a European war broke out.

In the work of propaganda, the commander of the German *Mittelmeer-Division*, Rear-Admiral Wilhelm Souchon, had played an important role, and the activities of the *Goeben* (supported by the German Military Mission) had more than counterbalanced the presence of a British Naval Mission.

In Souchon's own words:

'On 13 October, 1913, I had hoisted my flag at Trieste in *Goeben*. At the same time I had made it my job not only to visit and study all the naval bases and key points which might interest me, but also to see all the leading personalities with whom I might have dealings in case of war, whether as enemies or as companions in arms, or just friends.'

Clearly here was a leader of foresight.

Souchon was a remarkable man, a highly professional seaman with all the hallmarks of being an oustanding leader. His appearance was far from impressive; he was short in stature, with a stubbly beard and a Prussian hair-cut. His name indicated his French Huguenot origin, and to one close observer he combined the German passion for authority and thoroughness with much that was, in the Gallic fashion, genial and buoyant. To an American diplomat he seemed, off his quarter-deck, 'a droop-jawed,

[5] *Winston Churchill*, Vol. II.

determined little man in an ill-fitting frock coat, looking more like a parson than an admiral'. But from such outwardly unpromising material, events were to conjure up a hero—and Germany could rightly be proud of his personal achievement.

Even after Sarajevo the German government did nothing to ensure Turkish assistance if war came. The German Ambassador in Constantinople, Freiherr Hans von Wangenheim, was tepid towards any warlike alliance, but was overruled by the insistent enthusiasm of the Kaiser, a position greatly fortified by the imminence of war in July.

By 2 August, the day of the German invasion of Belgium, von Wangenheim, prodded by the German Chancellor von Bethmann Hollweg, signed an alliance with Turkey. This was dependent on the condition that Turkey 'either can or will undertake some action against Russia worthy of the name'. The Ottoman cabinet as a whole was given no opportunity to confirm or contest this dangerous arrangement.

Only three men were involved, and all are important to this development. The Grand Vizier (or Prime Minister) was Prince Said Halim, a cultivated aristocrat of the old school; his was not a strong or decisive personality, and was easily manipulated by the others. He was not keenly pro-German. Talaat Bey, the Minister of the Interior, had started his extraordinary career as a telegraph operator, and had become a key figure (in a curious double sense) among the aggressive Young Turks. He was a strong nationalist, was known to be above bribery—a rare bird in this corrupt jungle. Henry Morganthau,[6] the shrewd American Ambassador and a powerful Anglophile, has left a vivid picture of this striking figure.

'His powerful frame, his huge sweeping back and his rocky biceps emphasized that natural mental strength and forcefulness which made possible his career.'

His consumption of both food and drink was prodigious. His

[6] His son, Henry Morganthau Jr, was prominent during the Second World War as Secretary of the Treasury in Roosevelt's Cabinet.

wrists, 'twice the size of an ordinary man's,' seemed to symbolize his authority, for he kept the telegraph key (with which he had once earned his living) beside him, and used it to call up friends and to summon subordinates.[7] Altogether this gypsy figure, probably in part Bulgarian, was gargantuan both in aspect and appetite. As Compton Mackenzie's letter-writing soldier might have said of him, 'This Terrible Turk is by all accounts a proper Bulgar'.

But the central figure, who was to play so powerful a role in the *Goeben's* fortunes was the youthful, enigmatic and ruthless Minister of War, Enver Pasha. This remarkable man, with his Kaiser-like moustache, 'his little hairdresser face' (in Harold Nicolson's waspish phrase) 'perked patiently above his Prussian collar' had been sent to Berlin in 1909 at the age of twenty-seven as Turkish Military Attaché. He has been described by one historian as 'one of the most inept and disastrous generals who ever lived'. Morganthau noted 'a remorselessness, a lack of pity, a cold-blooded determination . . . of which his pleasing manners gave no indication'. He was also aware of Enver's colossal vanity, with his nickname of 'Napoleonik'—the little Napoleon—and his habit of sitting in his own house between a picture of the French Emperor and one of Frederick the Great.

As it happened, he and Churchill had met at the German military manoeuvres at Würzburg in 1909. Churchill apparently took a liking to this young dictator in the making, and believed that his favourable view was reciprocated. However, there was to be little sign of any deep political rapport, for Enver was soon wooing the Germans, and Churchill, disillusioned, was writing to Lloyd George in 1911: 'What fools the Young Turks have been to put their money on Germany.'

Enver did nothing by halves. He had, early in his time as War Minister, dismissed a large number of Turkish officers in a single day, on the grounds of their being 'politically unsound'. An unexpected friendship had at first grown up between this *arriviste* minister and the German Emperor; but it had cooled after

[7] Morganthau, *Secrets of the Bosphorus*.

Wilhelm learned that Enver's predecessor had been shot in his presence. Political life in Turkey was seldom uneventful or safe, and in due course a number of Turkish leaders fulfilled the ancient saying that 'bloodthirsty and deceitful men shall not live out half their days'.

By 1914 the Kaiser's mercurial judgement had begun to turn against Enver.

But, personal relations aside, Enver in the weeks before the war was working steadily towards the alliance. He openly told von Wangenheim that the Young Turks required the security of support from one of the groups of Great Powers.

Enver's sympathies naturally lay with the likely victors of any future struggle between the Central Powers and the Entente— and he regarded the former as potentially the stronger in war. This was the practical reason why the Turks backed the Germans when the crisis came.

The next stage was reached once hostilities had broken out; the German General Staff called loudly for immediate Turkish intervention against Russia, and very soon afterwards, against France and Great Britain. On 3 August von Wangenheim was told by the Grand Vizier that he was opposed to overt action, in the hope of diminishing the risk that Britain might commandeer the battleship *Sultan Osman*. He was a little late, since orders from Churchill had been given that same day to do this very thing. In Britain the stable door had been slammed just in time.

The prizes for which the Turks had worked so hard and paid so much were of enormous tactical and strategic value by any standards. They were two super-dreadnoughts which were all but completed, and already named *Sultan Osman I* and *Rashadieh*. The former was equipped with a prodigious, in fact a unique, main armament of fourteen 12-inch guns, with a designed speed of 22 knots. Their cost, which was vastly greater than today's values imply, had been partly paid to the tune of £3,600,000. This money had been extracted by village collections, a special tax on bread, and boxes placed on busy bridges around Constantinople. Women had even made an offering of their own hair. It would be easy to sentimentalize over the loss of countless piastres from Anatolian peasants—but we now know that Churchill's seemingly high-handed action was more justified than even he could then appreciate. It has lately been revealed that on 1 August, Enver and Talaat had offered to direct the *Sultan Osman* to a German North Sea port, and the Wilhelmstrasse had warmly accepted this proposal. The manner of their sequestration was abrupt and without immediate apology. Churchill wrote long afterwards a trifle optimistically that so far from making Turkey an enemy, his action nearly made her an ally.

In the northern waters of Tyneside and Barrow events were moving towards an anti-climax. Admiral Limpus had worked hard to turn 500 ill-educated conscripts into a crew for the *Sultan Osman*, and they reached Armstrong's yard early in 1914. This ship had originally been ordered by the Brazilian Navy—but the contract had lapsed. This led to one comic episode, since the usual lavatory arrangements appropriate to Brazilian (or European) custom had to be altered. All the lavatory bowls were torn out of the 'heads'—and replaced by facilities for the Turkish practice of squatting.

On 7 July the *Sultan Osman* moved down river for her trials with 200 dockyard mateys on board. After dry-docking at Devonport, where her seven main turrets caused some stir (the new *Queen Elizabeth* class had only four), her fitting out was completed. On her speed trials she reached 22.42 knots, this being a trifle above her designed speed. Not till 22 July was she berthed once more at her Tyneside yard. Some weeks earlier hints had been dropped by the Admiralty to both Armstrongs and Vickers that there was no need to hurry the completion of these two ships. The end of the road was reached on 27 July when a grubby Turkish ship arrived with the remainder of her crew. The handover was due on 2 August, and the fourteenth huge 12-inch gun was only shipped a day ahead of this. But still there was no sign of ammunition.

Meantime the First Lord had been exercising his powerful mind, and on the last day of July came a letter to the builders:

'As a result of consultations with the Law Officers of the Crown, Messrs Armstrong should be informed that in view of present circumstances, the Government cannot permit the ship to be handed over to a Foreign Power . . . or to leave their jurisdiction.'[8]

This was the end of the Turkish pipe-dream. Armstrongs called in the military, and on 1 August there were armed guards at the dockyard gates. With Britain's entry to the war but two days away, a company of Sherwood Foresters with fixed bayonets marched on board and there was little that the Turks could do. With their bright hopes of a splendid triumph dashed, nothing remained but to take to their transport and depart.

A bloodless victory had been achieved and the secret plan to sail her to Germany was frustrated. But there was a stiff price to be paid. Just as the invasion of 'gallant little Belgium' had united a largely pacific Liberal Cabinet in Britain, so the sequestration of the two great battleships, just before their departure to create the new Turkish Navy, united the Turks in a frenzy of anti-British emotion. One of Enver's problems, a psychological one, was solved, and a savage press campaign found an eager response. The other problem, that of replacement, appeared insoluble in the crucial first week of August.

It is necessary to move a few days ahead to see how hard Churchill tried to offset the bitterness engendered by his apparently high-handed action. He shortly made what seemed a handsome offer to Enver : that Turkey should receive at the end of the war either the two requisitioned Dreadnoughts, fully repaired, or else their full value; and in either case Britain would pay Turkey £1,000 a day in weekly instalments for every day she kept them. The arrangement would be effective from the day that all the German crew members had left Turkish territory for good, and would last so long as Turkey remained neutral. But the offer was too late, if not too little. Soon Sir Louis Mallet, the British Ambassador, who had counselled Whitehall against any impolitic

8 Hough, *The Big Battleship*.

or precipitate action and implored Grey to exercise patience, had to report that the farce was virtually played out.

One thing is certain—neither the prescient First Lord, nor any diplomatic or naval expert had any concept of the Turkish responses to a ticklish situation.

Writing nine years later, Churchill recorded that he could recall 'no great sphere of policy about which the British Government was less completely informed than the Turkish'. No wonder his resentment at being so seriously disillusioned spilled over in bitter words against 'scandalous, crumbling, decrepit, penniless Turkey'.

On 11 August the Grand Vizier, still hoping to achieve some degree of outward neutrality, requested that Admiral Limpus and his Naval Mission should remain and continue to assist the Turks. But this attitude could not last—and four days later the Mission was ordered to withdraw from the Turkish Fleet.

Limpus's future was the source of bitter debate in Whitehall. Churchill, in spite of some reservations as to Limpus's abilities, wanted him to be put immediately in charge of the Eastern Mediterranean Squadron. But Mallet had persuaded Grey at the Foreign Office that, in spite of his special knowledge of the Dardanelles and of Turkish naval affairs in general, it would be provocative to appoint Limpus. If he was passed over, said Mallet, it would convince the Turks that Britain still wanted peace. This was 'appeasement' with a vengeance.

Churchill was naturally furious and sent an angry protest to Grey—but to no avail. The Foreign Office overruled the First Lord on this essentially naval issue, and Limpus took over the post of Admiral-Superintendent, Malta Dockyard, in place of Vice-Admiral Carden.

It remains a moot point whether Limpus, who was essentially a staff officer, would have done better at the Dardanelles than Carden, who had a nervous breakdown three days before the main naval assault in March, 1915.

All these apparent changes of heart by the Turks must be counted as evidence of superior German diplomatic activity. Von

Wangenheim was a formidable figure physically, nicknamed 'the Cuirassier diplomat'. Morganthau has described him in vivid terms—'his huge, solid frame, his Gibraltar-like shoulders, erect and impregnable, his bold defiant head, his piercing eyes, the whole physical structure constantly pulsating with life'. He was indeed a tough personality, and expert in alternating suavity and aggression. Early in his career he had fought a duel with a man whom he suspected of being his wife's lover, and had 'shot out a kidney', according to Sir Maurice Bowra's *Memoirs*. History does not relate the clinical outcome.

His opposite number, Sir Louis Mallet, who had replaced a much less competent ambassador, did his best to convey the erratic drift of official Turkish sentiments. Yet according to one knowledgeable observer, Sir Edwin Pears, 'his inexperience heavily handicapped British diplomacy in Turkey'.

According to T. E. Lawrence, the failure on our diplomatic front was due to our embassy dragoman, Gerald Fitzmaurice, the fortunate possessor of 'an eagle-mind and personality of iron vigour'. Although he knew everything, he was (in Lawrence's view) 'a rabid R.C.' who hated all Jews and thus naturally regarded as the devil the Young Turk movement, which was (he said) '50 per cent crypto-Jew'. As a result Fitzmaurice 'threw the whole influence of England over to the unfashionable Sultan and his effete palace clique'. Owing to his prestige, the embassy staff (including Mallet) 'went down before him like ninepins. Thanks to him we rebuffed every friendly advance the Young Turks made.'

Lawrence's judgement may be suspect on many matters, but this opinion cannot be ignored entirely. It helps to account for so dismal a failure in face of powerful diplomacy by Germany. As it happened the Foreign Office grew alarmed at Fitzmaurice's anti-German views, and shortly before the final explosion, when his expertise might have been invaluable, he was recalled.

As to Turkey's own actions and reactions, there was much hurried improvisation. At the beginning of August nothing had been confirmed in writing—there was merely a hasty oral agreement between Wangenheim, Liman and Enver. The latter now started overtures with the Russian Military Attaché in Constantinople as an elaborate bluff. He tried to persuade the Russians that the mobilization of the Turkish army was not directed against them. St Petersburg was not so gullible as to accept this saucy disclaimer at its face value. Clearly there were a few Allied diplomats who saw Enver for the unprincipled twister that we can now so easily recognize.

The order from the German Admiralty for the *Goeben* to sail to Constantinople, closely followed a request by both Liman and Wangenheim after their conference on 1 August. They had elaborated the case showing the enormous advantages that would accrue if *Goeben* and *Breslau* joined the Turkish Fleet in the Black Sea. This was a classic understatement, when the Ottoman Navy was so negligible a force, even against the Russians. However, the Turkish leaders were not of one mind about how to receive the German ships when they reached the Dardanelles. Enver had issued orders to keep the Straits open for Souchon. But the Grand Vizier's authority contradicted Enver, and this caused undue alarm in Berlin; so the Germans sent a cautionary telegram to Souchon. This read: 'At the present time your call Constantinople not yet possible for political reasons'; it was received at Messina on 6 August and wisely ignored. This decision by Souchon was one of the most important in a confused and confusing week. The news of the apparent volte-face, due to contradictory opinions, reached Berlin belatedly, and Souchon not at all. All these delays were mainly due to problems of communication, since the science of wireless telegraphy was still in its infancy.

In the small hours of 6 August the Grand Vizier told Wangenheim that, though Turkey was still neutral, the cabinet had 'unanimously' (so he claimed) decided to open the Straits to Souchon and even to any Austrian ships. Some tough bargaining ensued, but Wangenheim quickly clinched the deal, lest any debate should compromise Souchon's squadron. As though he was not already doing his utmost, Wangenheim now received a sharp prod from Bethmann Hollweg to secure prompt Turkish intervention. The German Chancellor was sure that the arrival of the two German ships would immediately tip the scales—but this hope proved too optimistic. In the event Souchon's arrival in Turkish waters caused something like panic in the capital. There were divided counsels and, on the spot, total lack of direction. Even Enver was the victim of cold feet, until he in turn was prodded by some of his German staff.

Looking ahead, it is easier to assess the continued blindness in high places in Britain towards the stern realities of the Turkish situation. After war had broken out at last in November between Turkey and the Allied powers, it was still wishfully believed that all was not lost. As late as March, 1915, the formidable Director of Naval Intelligence, Captain W. R. Hall, acting on his own authority, attempted without success to buy off the Turkish Government with a mere £4 million. Ill-founded optimism could scarcely be carried to greater lengths—yet the perpetrator of this manoeuvre was one of the best Service brains in the country.

Not that the Germans, with their Prussian approach, were popular with the Turks. The basic gulf remained fixed; and the current gibe—'Deutschland über Allah'—was no indication of local love for the recently imported German ally. In fact, reports continued to reach Britain that many of Constantinople's most influential citizens would 'welcome an immediate break with the Germans, who had never been loved and were no longer trusted. Prayers were being offered up in the mosques for our arrival.'[9]

But these developments lay some months ahead.

Making every allowance for most difficult circumstances, it was clumsy British diplomacy—not so much in Constantinople as in Whitehall—which cold-shouldered Turkey into the embrace of Germany. But to the local populace it must have seemed that Allah himself had intervened, with the miraculous appearance off the Golden Horn of two splendid German warships.

[9] Sir William James, *The Eyes of the Navy.*

5

Souchon's Initiative

'Thank God the enemy does not know of our parlous situation.' ADMIRAL SOUCHON

WHEN war became imminent in the Mediterranean, the protagonists seemed unevenly matched to an absurd degree. Germany could not count on any effective naval support from Austria, though her fleet imposed a threat during the week before she was at war. Italy, though nominally associated with Germany, seemed, not for the last time in her history, to be prudently awaiting developments—a highly dubious ally. Turkey was totally devoid of any effective fleet, ancient or modern, and seemingly without any hope of acquiring one. This left the Central Powers with a grand total of two ships, the *Goeben*, and her slender, fast consort, the *Breslau*.

Ranged against her were the combined fleets of France and the Royal Navy. The French had a somewhat mixed bag of heavy ships, but these included a formidable total of twelve battleships, even though some were far from modern. The British fleet was large, varied and mostly of recent vintage. It included three earlier, but magnificent, battle cruisers, completed between 1908 and 1911. One of these ships, the *Indomitable*, had an impressive gunnery record; according to Admiral Fisher's boyish report she had, while steaming at 20 knots, 'hit a target one quarter her own size being towed on an unknown course at 12 knots at a distance of 5 miles, *18 times* out of 20! with her 12-inch guns!'

These battle cruisers displaced around 17,000 tons (6,000 less than *Goeben*) and had a designed speed of over 25 knots. Their belt armour was up to 6 inches, and they were armed with 8×12-inch and 16×4-inch guns. A second category in the fleet comprised four armoured cruisers of 14,600 tons, with a main armament 4×9.2-inch and 10×7.5-inch guns, and a speed of $21\frac{1}{2}$ knots. These last made up the First Cruiser Squadron under Rear-Admiral E. C. T. Troubridge, flying his flag in HMS *Defence*. There were also four light cruisers with a varied armament of 6-inch and 4-inch guns, and a speed of 25 knots. Finally there were four divisions of relatively slow, coal-burning, 26-knot destroyers—making a total flotilla of sixteen, with the old cruiser *Blenheim* as a depot ship. These small ships were apt to be chronically short of fuel.

It takes little imagination to sense how overwhelming the Allied fleet must have appeared, whether to friend or foe. In short, the German's single capital ship must contend with fifteen Allied capital ships, heavily supported by fast, light forces. By any standards Souchon faced a daunting—a seemingly impossible —task.

The joint pre-war strategy between France and Britain was distinctly muddled. There had been various conferences at a high level, including an impressive affair in Malta in 1912, attended by Asquith, Churchill, the GOC-in-C, the Governor, and the indispensable Captain Hankey. But details were left curiously vague, and phrases such as 'combined action if possible for the purposes of general engagement' did not suggest a clear intent. Practical matters, vital to any effective joint action, including the exchange of joint signal books and cyphers, were left undone or incomplete. It was, however, agreed that, in the event of war, with France and Britain as allies, then the overall command would devolve on a French Admiral. This in turn was to lead to foreseeable confusion, since the most senior French flag officer was junior to Milne, and so the latter would have, at the crucial moment, to be replaced. The seeds of muddle had been sedulously sown.

We have already seen how war came speedily, but not simultaneously, to the great powers. France was at war with Germany on 3 August. Her naval strength was concentrated on bringing her troops in North Africa from Algerian ports to Toulon. At this stage Milne was not yet permitted to enter into communication with the French admiral.

'Your first task', Churchill ordered him on 30 July, 'should be to aid the French in transportation of their African Army by covering, and, if possible, bringing to action individual fast German ships, particularly *Goeben*, who may interfere with that transportation.'

This was the first operative section of a signal whose latter part was to cause such costly confusion by its ambiguity—but consideration of this must be deferred for the moment.

The disposition of the fleets on 2 August may now be summarized : *Goeben* was at Brindisi, at the entrance to the Adriatic, to be shadowed by two British battle cruisers. 'Approach to Adriatic', ran the Admiralty signal, 'must be watched by cruisers and destroyers'; Milne himself was told to remain near Malta. So Troubridge sailed from Malta for the Adriatic with *Indomitable* and *Indefatigable* plus the First Cruiser Squadron, *Gloucester*, and eight destroyers. *Chatham* remained to watch the Straits of Messina, and the next day she was ordered to go right through the Straits to find out where the Germans were. In fact no enemy warships remained at Messina.

The initiative no longer lay with the British, in spite of their large superiority in ships. The whole issue turned on the conflict of duties, as between assisting the French in the West, bottling up the Austrians in the Adriatic, and finding and attacking the *Goeben*. The first clear move to achieve the latter objective came in a signal from the Admiralty at 6.30 pm on 3 August :

'The two battle cruisers must proceed to Straits of Gibraltar at high speed ready to prevent *Goeben* leaving Mediterranean.'

It is now time to trace the moves that the *Goeben* and the *Breslau* had already made. Souchon's own account, virtually

49

unknown and only available in a French translation, is our best guide. With only rare lapses, he is a remarkably objective chronicler of his own triumphant voyages.

He begins his narrative by a short account of his two ships.

'The *Goeben* and *Breslau* were both magnificent modern ships. The first had been launched only in 1911 at Hamburg, and was a large capital ship of 23,000 tons and of 52,000 HP, a speed of 29 knots [this figure may be an exaggeration as her *designed* speed was 25.5] and a principal armament of 10 × 11-inch guns. The second was a light cruiser launched also in 1911, of 4,500 tons, 25,000 HP, a speed of 27 knots and armed with 12 × 4.1-inch guns. The *Goeben* was accepted as being the fastest battleship or cruiser then in the Mediterranean. But that was no longer true in the summer of 1914. The *Goeben* had boilers which leaked, and this greatly reduced her speed and also her range of action. The *Moltke* was due to replace her in October.'

One feature her admiral did not mention was the austerity of her fittings—her wardroom lacked sofas, armchairs and pictures. Clearly this was a highly 'functional' ship of war. Souchon goes on to describe his reasons for infrequent contacts with 'the English'.

'In the relatively short time before the outbreak of war, it was impossible to meet them. I did not aim to visit them in Malta, as I knew the port of Valetta for a long time. If we didn't meet that was due to a principle closely followed by the English, to avoid staying with their ships at the same time as ours in foreign ports. The English admiral [Milne] never failed to appear pretentiously with several ships in all the ports we were about to leave, so as to efface the impression we had produced. John Bull always wanted "to spit in the soup"—as a marginal note by the Kaiser observed expressively on my reports.'

He then comes to the moment when he heard of the assassination of the arch-ducal couple, with whom he had lately enjoyed 'strawberry punch at their cosy little palace'.

'I at once had the feeling that this infamous outrage could lead Germany into war, and I was oppressed by the fear that I would perhaps be forced to commence this war with a flag-ship whose damaged boilers would compromise its efficiency. All my efforts ought therefore, above all, to be bent towards the replacement of these damaged tubes in the naval port of Pola in Austria.'

Through the Berlin authorities he ordered as many tubes as possible, with experienced workmen to install them.

'On board the *Goeben* we then settled down with zeal to this task, and in spite of the July heat the teams worked day and night; as a result, when the ship reached Messina it was possible to maintain a speed of 18 knots, with frequent slaking of the fires in certain boilers . . . It was possible under pressure of necessity to log 24 knots on 4 August.'

Souchon writes in the warmest terms of his debt to his chief engineer.

'For him there were no obstacles and he feared no responsi-bilities. Tireless himself, always alert and charming, he was a well-loved chief who understood how to get the best out of his men, his fuel, and his machines.'

Here are the clear signs of 'a happy ship'. *Goeben*, he continues,

'was the last warship to leave Durazzo. She had there estab-lished the most friendly relations with the light cruiser *Gloucester*, who proved our chief opponent in peaceful matches of water-polo.'

After a rendezvous with *Breslau* at Brindisi on 1 August, the two ships reached Messina in Sicily on 2 August.

'On board, the work proceeded as before. We achieved the change of boiler tubes, and put them in working order. In my cabin I discussed with my Chief of Staff the opportunities of taking an active part in the war. Nearly all the factors which were relevant to our projects were not, and could not be, determined—such as the probable attitude of our French and English adversaries, any pressure from our Italian and Austrian allies, a declaration of neutrality by Spain and Greece, the workings of our intelligence service, and what help we could expect from Germany. First, one could only consider that, on the one hand, there existed an unquestionable and crushing superiority of force, and on the other our two gallant ships were abandoned and alone.

'In these conditions the first idea was to carve a way to the North Sea. But the *Goeben's* damaged boilers forced us to give this up. Our chance of inflicting an effective injury on the enemy in the Mediterranean appeared very poor, even in the best circumstances. These did not seem likely to improve when the nations, whether neutral or at war, were identified. Also we did not care to wait at Pola on events. The hour demanded action, pursuit of the enemy, the neglect of no chance of fighting at once, even if failure meant being honourably sunk, for we had no assurance of trying again on the morrow!'

It is of some interest that Souchon (if we accept the accuracy of his post-war narrative) was inclined to treat the threat imposed by twelve French battleships in a quite cavalier fashion. These capital ships were of course old and slow—and Souchon rightly had a high regard for the dominance he could achieve by speed.

But his plan to attack the Algerian ports of embarkation, without any accurate intelligence as to the location of the French fleet, was bold to a degree. The bombardment was certain to be reported instantly by French wireless stations in Africa, and thus to attract, or at least alert, the enemy—possibly including Milne's battle cruisers.

'Through the night, with a storm ahead, the lights of the ships masked, oilskins on deck, canvas over the between-decks, the men carried out their routine tasks, fortified in spirit

1. Admiral Sir Berkeley Milne, Commander-in-Chief, Mediterranean

2. Admiral Sir Ernest Troubridge, Rear-Admiral Commanding First Cruiser Squadron, 1914

3. Rear-Admiral Wilhelm Souchon, Commanding the Mittelmeer-Division (*Goeben* and *Breslau*) in 1914

4. Admiral of the Fleet Lord Fisher, First Sea Lord 1904–10 and 1914–15

5. SMS *Goeben* flying the German ensign

6. *Yavuz* flying the Turkish ensign

against whatever Messina might bring us. In the narrow, stifling cabin my ADC brought me the telegram he had decyphered: "Danger of war imminent".'

Souchon instructed him to keep the order for mobilization secret for the moment. He then asked how many boilers were out of use.

' "Two during the period from 16.00 to 20.00 hours; one during this watch." "Damn" [There were 24 boilers in all.] To have under one's feet so lovely and powerful a ship, and to be like a shackled convict dragging a ball and chain at this moment—when the time for greatness is come, when your Kaiser appeals to you, when your comrades and kin think of you with fierce pride. Thank God the enemy does not know of our parlous situation. The *Goeben* is always taken to be the fastest ship in the Mediterranean.'

This was no idle boast, for *Goeben*'s reputation was widely accepted, and this nominal superiority, enhanced both by bluff and by prodigies in her boiler-rooms, made a vital contribution to her escape. Both the British admirals expected her to be able to steam away from (or around) her pursuers.

But Souchon was at all times a realist.

'We must act quickly before our wretched state gets known. Forward! and let us achieve all that our men and machinery can give, so long as we have fuel, water and shells. Obstacles are only there to be overcome, and we shall see who is the strongest ... It is not in vain that we have worked for thirty years as no fleet had worked, under the drive of the All Highest ... Let us rejoice that we are alive at this great moment! The more numerous the enemy the greater our share of honour! Forward!'

And in the same aggressive vein, Souchon tells of the frenzy of joy all around as the crew were now told of the order for mobilization, with 'music on deck, the Prussian march, Fredericus Rex!'

53

'As we expected we found neither Austrians or Italians when we arrived at Messina. The Italian Government had been shameless enough in their treachery hurriedly to forbid all their ports to deliver coal or victuals to us. We did not plead much. We simply helped ourselves by accosting German ships from which we coaled, though not without difficulties, of course, since their bunkers were not arranged to facilitate coaling.'

Souchon tells of many peacetime experiences of coaling under difficult conditions, and treating it as a sporting contest.

'But the coaling at Messina, influenced by the declaration of war, bettered all that I have seen. In the twinkling of an eye, axes and chisels had made everything vanish that could obstruct coaling; and the men went to work with such zeal, such spirit, that it took an effort on my part not personally to seize a shovel. Sweat dripped from everyone. The coal was unhappily unworthy of these brave efforts. Merchant ships use the cheapest coal, their boilers do not need the special quality necessary for a warship . . . particularly for the *Goeben*. But still this coal was better than none. What we took from the Hamburg liner *General* was fairly good.

'This fine ship of the German East Africa Line, full of passengers and freight for the Exhibition at Dar-es-Salaam, had been summoned by telegraph by me, and I had requisitioned her as a tender. She arrived at Messina at the same time as we did. I went on board and ordered the passengers off her. They said warm farewells to us soon, when their ferry passed close to us. We used the *General*, whether for materials, or to embark whatever stores could be removed for war. She followed me very cleverly to Constantinople and gave great and varied service during the whole war.

'My operational plan was quickly settled: to bombard the chief points of embarkation of the XIX Corps of the French army on the coast of Algeria, which were the fortified ports of Bône and Philippeville, and to demolish as fully as possible their equipment and shipping. To reach the Algerian coast at dawn on 4 August, the ships left Messina secretly at 1 am on the 3rd. Just before we weighed, we got news that war had been declared with France.'

As they moved north through the Straits, they passed Scylla and Charybdis. Souchon's odyssey had begun.

6

Brief Encounter

'*The tortures of Tantalus.*' CHURCHILL

A S Souchon neared the targets selected for attack in Algeria, he received by wireless at 2.35 am what was to prove one of the most important and effective signals of the war. This message, which much later was decyphered by Room 40, the cryptographic centre in the Admiralty Old Building, read: 'Alliance with Turkey. *Goeben* and *Breslau* proceed immediately to Constantinople. (Signed) Admiralty Staff of Navy.' Souchon's post-war comment on this was:

> 'The idea of turning about, so short a time before that moment so ardently wished by us all, before opening fire—my heart could not accept that. Keeping to our programme, the first German projectiles whistled through the dawn on to quays and transports, sowing death and panic among the assembled troops, on their way to France.'

The facts are a trifle less dramatic, as there were few troops and no transports to hit.

But this order and its implication of Turkish complicity—with undreamed-of visions of her rising to become a full ally of Germany—cannot fail to have stirred Souchon and his men to fantastic endeavours, as events were soon to prove.

In sharp contrast with Souchon's bold initiative, Milne with his far larger forces was faced with the unenviable, defensive exercise of trying to guess his opponent's plan. With so large a preponderance of ships this must seem a trifle odd if not positively wrong. But, as will later appear, Milne's dilemma was not wholly the product of his own limited imagination.

The *Goeben* and *Breslau* had reached Messina at 1 pm on

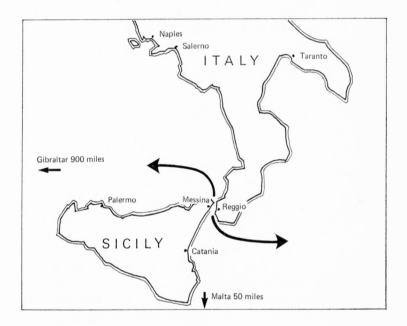

2 August. But this vital intelligence did not reach Milne till the early hours of 3 August. His mind was filled with his Admiralty's instructions to protect convoys to the west, to prevent a breakout past Gibraltar, and to stop Souchon from meeting a collier believed to be at Palma in Majorca. With the number of ships at his command, it has been thought strange that Milne did not attempt to block, or at least watch, both ends of the Straits of Messina. The Straits run north and south; but the northern exit leads in effect to the west, while the southern end leads directly to the east. This piece of topography, so obvious from

a glance at the map, governed all the plans and counter-plans, now and later, which centred on Messina.

So Milne's over-riding duty, as he saw it, concerned controlling the northern end. He knew from the *Chatham* that no ships had been found at Messina, very soon after he had learned that the *Goeben* and *Breslau* had been there the day before. Anxious above all to prevent any westward move, he sent (early on 3 August) a large force of two battle cruisers and three armoured cruisers south of Sicily towards the west. He did not aim at blocking the actual northern exit, right up to the six-mile limit, perhaps since this meant steaming all the way round the western tip of Sicily. Souchon, however, assumed that Milne's ships were probably so placed. By 6.30 pm the Admiralty decided that the main risk was the breakout of the German ships into the Atlantic, and sent a signal to this effect. At 9 pm Milne ordered *Indomitable* and *Indefatigable* to proceed at 22 knots to Gibraltar ready to prevent *Goeben* leaving the Mediterranean. Their only consort, the light cruiser *Chatham*, was detached and told to rejoin the flag. Milne, acting on orders, stayed in his flagship, *Inflexible*, near Malta to co-ordinate his widely dispersed fleet. For the moment everything hinged on a declaration of war with Germany. Captain Kennedy in *Indomitable* was now the senior officer of this formidable searching force. It is a significant fact that when Kennedy was first appointed to command his battlecruiser he asked the Commander-in-Chief to allow him to see the relevant Admiralty War plans; but this Milne refused to do.

The *Indomitable* and *Indefatigable* were now heading almost due west. Kennedy's crisp official report (here slightly abbreviated) tells the story of what followed:

'4 August

10.32 am. Sighted *Breslau* on starboard steering to eastward at high speed.

10.34 am. Sighted *Goeben* on port bow at about 17,000 yards, steering easterly at about 20 knots. She was cleared for action but her guns were laid fore and aft. Went to action stations. *Goeben* altered course to (her) port as if to close us or cross close to our bows. We altered to starboard, she then ported and we passed each other at about 8,000 yards. She proceeded on her easterly course and we then gradually turned round to port keeping our broadside on her. She turned to port also and we continued till she was heading east when she proceded on that course at about 20 knots. We took station astern of her about 11,000 yards to 7,000 yards, *Indefatigable* on our quarter at first and then on our beam.

About Noon. *Goeben* decreased speed. We did also—12.50 pm. She went on again and we went 20 knots. At about 11.0 am we on the bridge lost sight of *Breslau* to the northward, but she was reported from our Fore Control up to about 11.30 am. We gave all our attention to the Battle Cruiser. We heard *Breslau* calling up a W/T Station.

2.25 pm. *Breslau* joined *Goeben* and they and we proceeded at full speed.

3.0 pm. Joined by *Dublin*. Ordered her to form on starboard beam of *Goeben* and keep out of gun range. Proceeded at full speed to endeavour to close *Goeben* and appeared to be slightly overtaking her. Sent hands to tea at 3.30 pm. and *Indefatigable* to go to tea after us.

3.45 pm. *Goeben* and *Breslau* appeared to be going away from us fairly rapidly, our revolutions only 249. Horizon very misty to eastward.

4.0 pm. *Goeben* only just in sight. Ordered Engine Room to go as fast as possible. *Indefatigable* 2 points before port beam. Ordered her to keep Germans in sight. She drew ahead in bearing, also *Dublin* on Starboard bow, 5 miles. Revolutions only 240.

4.35 pm. Lost sight of *Goeben*.'[1]

The pursuit had lasted for six hours.

It may be puzzling how the *Goeben*, with her damaged boilers,

[1] Lumby.

managed to evade her three pursuers. She had, so Souchon claimed after the war, a trial speed of 29 knots, though her alleged 'designed' speed was only 25.5 knots. The *Indomitable* class were also designed to reach 25.5 knots; but it was some time since the British cruisers had been in dry dock, and their engine room staff were short of a wartime establishment. The *Goeben*, too, had not been drydocked for ten months. So each party could reasonably claim to be far below par. Some of the speeds logged in both pursuits were manifestly, though unwittingly, false. There are numerous contradictions which do not matter, except that they make the reader of the original signals a trifle confused!

It was a little ironic that the turbines in the *Goeben* were British, being designed and made by Parsons; in confusing contrast, the British ships carried armour made by Krupp.

Souchon's version, written after the war, is by comparison highly coloured.

'The *Goeben* and *Breslau* had scarcely finished their task [of bombarding Bône and Philippeville] when the French shipping began to jabber like lunatics, in clear, so that, full of joy and pride, we knew that we had had success. Hereafter it was important to disappear as swiftly and discreetly as we had appeared. We did not succeed. We fell into the clutches of the British lion.

'At 10 am, there suddenly appeared, on the port bow, two huge warships. They are bow on to us and move at great speed. "Action stations." We hold our course ready to fire. What is going to happen? *Goeben*, all honour to your name, show what German gunners and German material are worth, even in face of superior numbers and weight of broadside. Poor, pretty, little *Breslau*, how will you come out of it?

'They approach each other rapidly, as we realise the position. These are not French ships with a big freeboard, but English tripod capital ships of the *Indomitable* class. We see them, with anguished attention, pass at 9,000 yards; but they don't fire, they turn about and begin to follow us. I don't dare to open fire as I don't know whether England is our enemy, and I am astonished that they don't fire. Yet the English start all their wars by falling on their enemy before any declaration, often in the middle of total peace.'

It would be interesting to question the admiral on this highly dubious bit of history—maybe he had got it from the All-Highest.

'The English battle cruisers merely attempt to jam our wireless systematically.

'We must act so that they won't notice that our boilers are defective, and must try to shake off contact with them. We achieve both these ends thanks to the almost superhuman efforts of our engineers, far superior to the British, and thanks to the lucky chance that the visibility was very poor in the evening. The English had launched in pursuit several light cruisers [in fact only the *Dublin*] which were all modern vessels of 25 or 26 knots. Although some boilers were constantly failing on the *Goeben* [as many as three at one time], the ship succeeded in producing at this moment enough revolutions for 23 knots; and thanks to that—wonder of wonders —we could get away from the English ships!'

One of *Goeben's* crew has left a grim picture of the scenes below :

'In the glow of the boiler-rooms and bunkers, heroic efforts were made. The whole ship's company, in so far as they were not indispensable for the guns or for duty on the bridge, were ordered to the bunkers and stokeholds to trim coal. Stokers, seamen, petty officers, midshipmen, officers, the whole personnel worked at trimming coal, stoking, and clearing the ash. The overheated air affected lungs and heart. Shut off from the outer air by the armoured deck, we worked in the compressed atmosphere forced down through the ventilators. The coal in the neighbourhood of the boilers could be left. That in the outlying bunkers was trimmed first, and in view of the great length of the ship these were often a long way from the boiler-room. For this reason all hands were called upon to help.

'There was an infernal din going on in the interior of the ship. The artificial draught roared and hissed from above into the stokeholds, drove into the open furnace doors, fanning the glowing coal, and swept roaring up the smoke-stacks. In the engine-room there was the whir of the turbines, revolving at ever-increasing speed; the whole ship trembled and quaked. The *Goeben* was going all out.'[2]

Souchon's biographer draws a flamboyant picture, as the admiral asks himself,

'Shall we salute? That is the crucial problem. Absolute peace prevails with our English cousins. As the junior in rank Souchon must act first. But at such a distance it is not at first possible to make out whether the leading ship flies Admiral Milne's flag or not.'[3]

In fact, there was no admiral's flag on either ship to salute; for Milne was in *Inflexible* off Malta; and Souchon, having flown the Russian flag as *Goeben* closed on Philippeville, as a *ruse de guerre*, omitted to fly his own.

On Milne's instructions, the last of his pursuing ships, the *Dublin*, turned back at 9.52 pm towards the west, while still 250 miles short of Messina. Milne's obsession with a now highly improbable escape towards Gibraltar continued to dominate his planning. He ordered a rendezvous next day off Pantellaria east of Cape Bon.

Churchill has left a famous account of how things looked in the Admiralty. On receiving the news of the *Goeben* and *Breslau* being shadowed, he signalled delightedly, 'Very good. Hold her. War imminent.'

'. . . Throughout this long summer afternoon', he wrote, 'three great ships, hunted and hunters, were cleaving the clear waters

[2] Georg Kopp, *Two Lone Ships*.
[3] M. E. Mäkelä, *Souchon der Goebenadmiral*.

of the Mediterranean in tense and oppressive calm. At any moment the *Goeben* could have been smitten at under 10,000 yards range by sixteen 12-inch guns firing nearly treble her own weight of metal. At the Admiralty we suffered the tortures of Tantalus.

'At about 5 o'clock Prince Louis observed that there was still time to sink the *Goeben* before dark. [He could not then know that contact had already been lost.] ... We hoped to sink her the next day. Where could she go? Pola seemed her only refuge throughout the Mediterranean. According to international law nothing but internment awaited her elsewhere. The Turks had kept their secret well.'[4]

To return to the conclusion of Souchon's first sally :

'Our night passage along the coast of Sicily led to another encounter, this time with a flotilla of torpedo-boats. Happily we were able just in time, by the light of the moon, to recognise them as Italians and hold our fire.

'The ships re-entered Messina in a state of extreme exhaustion. The men had scarcely slept; during their four hour watches they had been all the time alert at their posts, during their off duty they had shifted coal. We found a young sailor half-dead from exhaustion in a bunker. And further there could be no question of more rest. Our stay at Messina had to be as brief as possible; and in spite of the difficult circumstances, time must be used to the best advantage for coaling.'

[4] *The World Crisis.*

The Thrust to the East

'The combined effrontery, promptitude and sagacity of the move.' CORBETT

S OUCHON'S plan was now cut and dried—there remained only the slight problem of coaling twice in neutral or hostile waters, and evading a large and wide-spread British fleet.

The War Staff in Whitehall and the two admirals on the spot were in a more problematic position, hampered as they were by total ignorance of the Turkish alliance and delayed communications between London and the Commander-in-Chief. A further factor was the lack of rapport between Milne and Troubridge and the absence of co-ordination with their French allies.

We have seen the difficulties experienced by the newly formed War Staff and the First Lord. In the words of the official historian, Sir Julian Corbett, a man most reluctant to deliver ill-considered verdicts :

'The sudden pressure on an embryonic staff organization was more than it could bear, but the fact remains that intelligence essential for forming a correct appreciation of the shifting situation either did not reach [Milne], or reached him too late.'

The situation, as Milne examined it on the morning of 5 August after the declaration of war, was complex. He did not know positively until twenty-four hours later that the German ships were at Messina. There, the British consul's message to this effect had, unbelievably, to be passed to Milne via London and Malta. He himself was still preoccupied with the western escape route and was patrolling off Bizerta where some of his ships were coaling. In fact Captain Kennedy found that the coal briquettes which were ready for him were no good, and had to wait to requisition coal from a British collier, loaded pre-war for possible *German* use.

Apart from the problem posed by the Germans at Messina, there was the uncertainty about the Adriatic. The Austrians had a large force of out-of-date battleships, and it seemed only a matter of time before they went to war. It seemed to nearly all those concerned that Souchon must be thinking of linking up with the Austrian fleet, or even finding sanctuary in Pola. A message that mines had been laid and lights extinguished in the Dardanelles merely removed still further from Milne's mind the idea of Souchon making for Turkish waters.

Milne of course, as was his duty, relied on such directions as he had from the Admiralty, and we must now examine these. There were two of exceptional importance, and we now know that both were drafted in the First Lord's own hand. On 30 July, looking ahead at all the possibilities, Churchill told Milne, as has already been noted, that he must not be seriously engaged with Austrian ships before they knew what Italy would do, and that his first task should be to aid the French and bring to action individual fast German ships, particularly *Goeben*. The second part of the signal ran thus:

'Do not at this stage be brought to action against superior forces, except in combination with the French, as part of a general battle. The speed of your squadron is sufficient to enable you to choose your moment ... You must husband your strength at the outset.'

The latent ambiguities which this signal held will appear shortly, in spite of the author's modest comment:

'So far as the English language may serve as a vehicle of

thought, the words employed appear to express the intentions we had formed.'[1]

But, alas, they also failed to allow for the fog of doubt that developed quickly as the situation changed.

The second crucial signal, also in Churchill's own hand, was timed 12.50 am on 3 August, and read:

'Watch on mouth of Adriatic should be maintained, but *Goeben* is your objective. Follow her and shadow her wherever she goes and be ready to act on declaration of war, which appears probable and imminent. Acknowledge.'

So, on 5 August, Milne asked the Admiralty: 'Is Austria neutral power?' and was told:

'Austria has not declared war against France or England. Continue watching Adriatic for double purpose of preventing Austrians from emerging unobserved and preventing Germans entering.'

Milne's orders to Troubridge were:

'First Cruiser Squadron [comprising four armoured cruisers armed with 9.2-inch guns] and *Gloucester* [light cruiser] will remain watching entrance to Adriatic and are not to get seriously engaged with superior force.'

Troubridge signalled Milne (5 August):

'In case *Goeben* is in these waters I am keeping within Santa Maura [in modern terms, the island of Levkas]. If we encounter her I will attempt to draw her into narrow waters when I can engage her at our range.'

Milne replied:

'In case she should come out use destroyer flotilla night work. *Dublin* arrives Malta Thursday morning [6 August]; coals, will leave immediately join you with two destroyers.'

[1] *The World Crisis.*

At 6.10 pm on 6 August, the vital signal was sent by *Gloucester*, the only ship on watch at the southern outlet from the Straits of Messina, that *Goeben* and (seven minutes later) *Breslau* were under way, steering east. With Milne's heavy ships off the west end of Sicily, and short of coal, the prospects were not bright.

But we must return to Messina and discover what Souchon had achieved since returning from his first sortie thirty-seven hours earlier.

He had a sharp set-back at the outset. A signal to the Austrian admiral, Haus, asking for help had extracted the reply: 'The second stage of mobilization has produced demoralization. Unable to come.' This must have been somewhat frustrating, after Austria's eagerness to precipitate a war against Serbia at any cost. Later Haus excused himself, by saying that it was clearly hopeless to try to free the *Goeben* from the formidable Anglo-French grip, and so he had not made the attempt.

At Messina they neglected nothing to get hold of coal. The Italians gave permission 'for the last time'. German merchant ships vied with each other to hand over their coal, although they did not have the best coal or the most suitable means of discharging it. According to Souchon, his chief of staff

'even succeeded in getting us coal from an English ship, though not in the way that legend has suggested, by drinking the English captain under the table. Altogether we succeeded in getting 2,000 tons of coal. In spite of the exhaustion of the crew, and the heat of these August days, the transfer of coal went on day and night interminably. Hour by hour it went more slowly. Music in the form of martial airs, extra rations, stirring speeches, the example of those officers who worked along with them, my own encouragements, nothing could keep the men on their legs. When they collapsed from the effect of exhaustion, we sent them in turn to sleep for a few hours on the passengers' bunks in the *General*, we plied them with cool drinks and baths, but all in vain; the cases of fainting and sunstroke multiplied, the loading of coal came almost to a stop. With a heavy heart (for there was plenty of coal still to be transferred), I gave the order to raise steam at noon, on 6 August. I wished to weigh anchor at 5 pm, since the enemy awaited us. It was essential to have some rest before preparing for battle.'

There were rumours in Sicily of a large fleet off Taormina at the southern exit, but Souchon kept these messages to himself. He did not want the exhausted crew to have their weariness turned to despair. The locals were to show truly Latin hysteria.

'Numerous Sicilians, avid for sensation, besieged us night and day. People in rags offered to sell fruit, titbits, post cards and keepsakes of every kind; singers with mandolines, mouth-organs and castanettes; policemen, girls, monks, soldiers, sisters, and even some well-dressed people, tried untiringly to grapple with our half-naked, coal-blackened men, to pinch everything that was not riveted or nailed, from their jumper-buttons to shovel-handles, in memory of "those about to die". The noise of coaling, the whistle of steam, the din of wind-lasses, the grinding of shovels mingled with the dust, the steam, the smell of oil and sweat, and finally the cries of paper sellers with special posters: "Into the Jaws of Death" ... "The Last Departure" ... "Disgrace or Death" ... "The Perilous Leap to the Peak of Glory". More than anything we wanted a moment of rest to find a little quiet corner where one could steal an instant for thoughts of home, for writing some lines of farewell ... Legend tells of a long queue of men going ashore to the German consulate, with their last wills and with portraits of the Kaiser. This was entirely a fantasy.'

Souchon seized the opportunity of enlisting 400 extra men, sailors, waiters, colonials and so forth.

'A cabin boy of 15 assailed everyone with pleas and tears to be taken. He only stopped when he had seen me. A day or two later he was dragged, half-dead, from one of the *Breslau*'s bunkers.'

On 6 August, during the afternoon, everyone washed and rested, and the ship was made ready for battle; all who had them put on clean underwear and fresh clothes.

'At 11 am I received a telegram from the General Staff as follows: "For various reasons you should not enter Constantinople for the moment." This message did not make me hesitate in my determination to reach the Dardanelles, any more than the invitation from our Naval Attaché in Rome to enter the Adriatic. It was impossible for me to remain in the Mediterranean in face of the crushing superiority of the enemy, and, as a result, the total lack of any means of subsistence. I did not wish in any circumstances to sail into the Adriatic in the certainty that it would be very difficult for me to operate actively, as I would have to depend on the Austrians. Thus I firmly decided to enter the Dardanelles, if necessary against the will of the Turks, and to carry the war into the Black Sea. I hoped to carry the Turks with me in a war against their traditional enemy, the "Muscovite".

'For the success of the breakout I had to reckon on the fact that the enemy was unaware of our damaged boilers, and hence, of the reduced speed and range of action which resulted for the *Goeben*; that they were equally unaware of our destination, and that they had nothing available to stop us in that direction; and also, and above all—and this for me was rather an instinct than a certainty—that the English admirals of to-day would not challenge me unless they succeeded in bringing about the full superiority of all their concentrated forces.'

The implication that nothing would stop them going in the direction of Turkey suggests that *he* did not believe that Troubridge's cruiser squadron, unsupported, could cope—a significant judgement.

'The moon being full and the night clear, we had little fear of attacks by British destroyers. Everything depended, moreover, on the lead I could gain from my pursuers, on being able to meet at least one of the summoned lighters.

'My orders were very simple: "The *Goeben* will weigh at 5 pm speed 17 knots, the *Breslau* will follow at 5 miles distance. I will attempt to give the impression at first that we are aiming for the Adriatic—then if that works, I will make a wide turn to starboard, surreptitiously, during the night and gain distance with all speed in the direction of Cape Matapan."

'Our departure worked out as we had foreseen. The ships, filled with hope of victory, moved towards an uncertain prospect, cutting proudly through the water, with yells from a massed crowd . . . And all that in broad daylight and in sight of the cruisers [in fact the *Gloucester* alone] guarding the outlet.'

Souchon saw *Gloucester* take up her shadowing role and maintain it through the night which was clear, silent, and bright with moonlight. Every effort was made, even in those early days of wireless telegraphy, to jam the reports which they knew *Gloucester* would be constantly trying to transmit.

In fact, *Gloucester* was carrying out her primary duty of shadowing and reporting, without being brought to action, with superb skill and enterprise. For, as was obvious to both sides, *Goeben* could, if she chose, turn on her determined foe and blow her out of the water. Her signals, in spite of the jamming (which for technical reasons could not be continuous) came in a steady accurate stream: '6.10 pm *Goeben* steering east.' '6.27 pm Urgent. *Breslau* one mile astern of *Goeben*.' '6.28 Speed of enemy 26 knots.' (This was in excess of Souchon's claims.) '6.40 *Goeben* will round Spartivento [the toe of Italy] at 7.20 pm.' '6.54 pm Course of enemy E.S.E.' '7.26 pm Am being deliberately interfered with.' (We can guess that *Gloucester*'s captain, Howard Kelly, who had a mordant sense of humour, enjoyed drafting this pleasantry.) '8.30 pm *Goeben* and *Breslau* approximate course N 65 E, speed 18 knots.' After reporting that the two German ships had, for the time being, parted company, there came a signal of vital importance: '10.46 pm Urgent. *Goeben* altering course to southward.' And at midnight this was confirmed by a signal: 'Course S 54 E, speed 22 knots,' adding that her coal was down to 700 tons, with an expenditure at this speed of about 350 per day.

These admirably precise and positive messages were received by both Milne and Troubridge, and the latter reported his accurate conclusion to the Commander-in-Chief very early on 7 August: '*Goeben* is going towards Matapan.' At this moment (1 am) Troubridge, with his four armoured cruisers, was 140 miles away to the north, near the island of Paxos. The crisis of *Goeben*'s odyssey, as of Troubridge's career, was swiftly approaching.

In the *Goeben*, a grim boiler-room drama was being enacted. The successful evasion of the heavy ships, which Souchon was certain must be approaching in support of the *Gloucester*, required a supreme effort; and even sustaining 18 knots was a costly achievement. A member of the *Goeben*'s crew draws a Goya-like picture:

'In silence, but pluckily and undismayed, the stokers stuck to their work ... They served the fires, tearing open the furnace doors, trimming the coal, drawing out the ash, and putting the fresh coal ready. The sweat ran in streams down their gleaming torsos. The searing heat from the furnaces burned the skin and singed the hair. And still the work went on in the torrid stokeholds. It was here that the issue was being fought out ...

'At such a speed, damage to boiler-tubes was unavoidable. The material was not equal to these exorbitant demands. A stoker was scalded dangerously—and he was not the first. A silent, unostentatious heroism was being displayed. Any moment that dreadful uncanny hissing might be repeated, and spouts of steam and boiling water do their deadly work on men's bare bodies. Yet every man stuck to his job. Four heroes, four plucky shipmates, paid with their lives in that hell of toil for the *Goeben*'s break-through and the success of our exploit.'[2]

[2] *Two Lone Ships.*

8

Admiral Troubridge's Dilemma

'The terrible "If's" accumulate.' CHURCHILL

IN tracing the problems that confronted the Germans on the one hand and the Admiralty and Milne on the other, little has been said as yet of Admiral Troubridge's anxieties. For the British to succeed, everything turned on his ability to intercept the German ships. For a proper understanding of the story it is essential, as far as may be, to enter Troubridge's mind, to assess the problem as it confronted him and to appreciate which factors, now easily evident to us, were hidden at the time from him.

As Rear-Admiral Commanding the First Cruiser Squadron he was directly subordinate to the Commander-in-Chief. The latter could add ships to his junior's command—or subtract them—without discussion. The notorious telegram of 30 July from the Admiralty to Milne, has already been quoted. The crucial phrases were the instruction that his first task should be to aid the French, and, if possible, to bring to action 'individual fast German ships, particularly *Goeben*'. The message continued, 'Do not at this stage be brought to action against superior forces ... The speed of your squadron is sufficient to enable you to choose your moment.' This message was addressed to Milne and we may assume that the squadron in question comprised the three battle cruisers, not Troubridge's smaller and much slower cruisers. Their speed was quite insufficient to allow their admiral to choose his moment. In fact what Churchill had in mind, and it was his hand that drafted the telegram, was that

Milne could avoid engaging the twelve massive but relatively slow Austrian battleships—should these leave their Adriatic base and seek action.

In this context some senior commanders in the Mediterranean, though not Milne, were uncertain of the application of the dangerously vague phrase—'superior forces'. Vice-Admiral K. G. B. Dewar singled out this telegram as 'the principal factor in this almost incredible train of errors emanating from Whitehall'. Sir Julian Corbett wrote in the Official History: 'The order [of 30 July] was natural enough, but . . . it had very regrettable consequences.' Troubridge throughout these anxious days—and forever after—held strongly to the principle that (barring specific orders from his Commander-in-Chief), right or wrong, 'it is, to my judgement, solely the officer who is in the face of the enemy, who can decide what is a superior, and what is not a superior, force'.

Milne had, on 2 August, shown his second-in-command the 30 July telegram and emphasized that Troubridge was himself to be governed by its warning. He then had what he called 'a very considerable conversation' with Milne on this precise question of avoiding a superior force. At this stage Troubridge was further confused by the assumption—a most reasonable one— that as Milne was due to be superseded by a French admiral on the outbreak of war, the British command would at once devolve on him. This would of course imply a full authority in command, with absolute control of the disposition of ships, including the three powerful *Inflexibles*.

At Malta Troubridge called together all the captains in the Mediterranean Fleet (apart from Milne's Flag Captain), and told them of his intentions. He even specified that in certain circumstances 'they must not be surprised if they saw me with the squadron run away'. And he elaborated the special conditions, principally in narrow waters near land, in which he would endeavour to engage the *Goeben*.

'I had quite determined that I could not engage the *Goeben* in broad daylight with the visibility that prevails in the Adriatic, which is almost any distance from the masthead.'

During the night of 6/7 August Troubridge steamed north, having received evidence suggesting that the *Goeben* was aiming to enter the Adriatic; there were also rumours that the Austrian Fleet might be coming south, possibly to meet up with the *Goeben*. The admiral had to consider many conflicting possibilities. Later he said,

'I am not ashamed of these surmises. It is well known that Nelson's letters are full of pages of surmises of where the enemy is bound for when once she had left a port.'

As he told the subsequent Court of Enquiry, 'There are moments, Sir, when one feels one is asked almost too much.' He had decided on principle that he would avoid being brought to action by the *Goeben* in the open sea, where she could sight him at 25 or 30 miles.

At 12.30 am, after they had turned south, his Flag Captain, Fawcet Wray, went to see the admiral, to 'talk about the possibilities of the night'. Troubridge expressed his intention of going down to the southward (as Wray records it) 'to see what was going to happen'.

'The *Dublin* [a light cruiser commanded by John Kelly] had been ordered to attack, or rather to sink, the *Goeben*, on a bright moonlight night, and he thought there was a possibility, or he hoped there was a possibility, of her being winged; that is to say, her speed reduced, and there was a possibility of something happening in the way of [*Goeben*] turning to the Adriatic again.'

Reading the account of this conversation between two men, both frustrated and very short of sleep, one senses the baffling atmosphere of uncertainty—the true fog of war.

At the moment when Troubridge and Wray were in conference, the *Dublin* with two destroyers was under orders to intercept the *Goeben* for a night attack with torpedoes. Subsequent plotting shows that she probably passed within sight of her quarry; but it is thought that with the expectation of sighting the German ship on the port hand, all hands were looking out in that direction; but *Goeben* must in all likelihood have passed her to starboard. By chance *Dublin*'s commander, Captain John Kelly, was brother of the *Gloucester*'s captain.

Then, suddenly, Troubridge felt he could not sustain his plan of qualified evasion. As he put it to the two very senior admirals at the Court of Enquiry (Meux and Callaghan) in a frank and moving passage:

> 'You have both been in command of Fleets and Squadrons [though only in times of peace] and there is a moment when one feels that all might be lost ... the feeling that the long watch would be ended one way or another—in fact what is described colloquially as "bloody minded"—I felt I would fight her.'[1]

At about 2.45 am Troubridge was confronted with his Flag Captain's urgent query, 'Are you going to fight, Sir?' He answered, 'Yes. I know it is wrong, but I cannot have the name of the whole of the Mediterranean Squadron stink.'

Troubridge then dictated this signal to his Squadron:

> 'I am endeavouring to cross the bows of *Goeben* by 6 am, and intend to engage her if possible. Be prepared to form on a line of bearing turning into line ahead as required. If we have not cut him off I may retire behind Zante [the most southerly of the Ionian islands] to avoid a long-range action.'

Unhappily, shortly after this splendid and decisive commitment, there were second thoughts. Wray takes up the narrative.

> 'At about 3.30 am having thought for half an hour I concluded I did not like [the decision], and therefore it was my duty as Flag Captain to place my views before him. I went to

[1] Lumby.

76

the Rear-Admiral who had his lights out, but was awake. I said "I don't like it, Sir"; and he said, "Neither do I, but why?" I pointed out to him that the *Dublin* had obviously failed to accomplish her night torpedo attack, and the *Goeben* had not been winged; that the C-in-C had informed him that he was returning to Malta at slow speed without informing the Rear-Admiral of his instructions. I called attention to the visibility and said "I don't see what you can do. Two courses are open to the *Goeben*. 1. Directly on sighting you to circle round at radius of visibility, or 2. To circle round at some range outside 16,000 yards which her guns will carry and yours will not. [Wray was a notable gunnery expert.] It seems likely to be the suicide of the squadron." He said, "Are you sure we cannot close the range of guns," and I replied, "Yes, Sir, but we will send for the Navigator." Before I went for the Navigator the Rear-Admiral said, "I can't turn away now. Think of my pride." I said, "Does your pride count in a thing like this?"

After Troubridge had seen the navigating officer, Wray received a message :

' "The Rear-Admiral wishes us to alter course to S.30 E (i.e. 30° to port)," and then I saw what his decision was. Afterwards I went down to him and said, "Admiral, that was the bravest thing you have ever done in your life." '[2]

Some weeks later Wray was asked to describe Troubridge's general demeanour that night. Wray replied that from midnight till 2.45 'if I may use the expression, I should call him "bloody minded" '. At 3.30 he seemed very worried. When Wray came back and told him how much he approved his decision to abandon the chase, 'I think he was in tears.' Thus ended a confrontation between an Admiral and his Flag Captain possibly without precedent in the annals of the Royal Navy.

It would be wrong to ignore the great changes in service
[2] Lumby.

relationships during the past fifty years. The gulf between an Admiral and his Flag Captain in 1914 was wider and more inflexible than can easily be understood today. Nevertheless it seems almost incredible that Troubridge should have been planning—at least temporarily—to cross the *Goeben's* bow at 6 am, without any full discussion of detailed tactics with his flag captain. If Wray had not initiated the dialogue on three separate occasions, between midnight and 3.30 am, how long, one wonders, would Troubridge have delayed issuing orders.

So the sad signal was sent at 4.05 am to the Commander-in-Chief:

'Being only able to meet *Goeben* outside the range of our guns and inside his I have abandoned the chase with my squadron request instructions for light cruisers. *Goeben* evidently going to Eastern Mediterranean. I had hoped to have met her before daylight.'

Wray then realized to his surprise that his admiral was giving up not just his plan to lie across the *Goeben*'s bows but was not even going to join the *Gloucester* in shadowing the Germans. He claims that he was horrified.

By 10 am Troubridge had reached the shelter of Zante, where on his instructions his destroyers joined him. It appears doubtful if they had enough coal to attempt a torpedo attack.

Not unreasonably Milne, who was approaching Malta from the west to coal his battle cruisers, signalled:

'Why did you not continue to cut off *Goeben*. She was only going 17 knots [This was an accurate and up-to-date report from *Gloucester*.] and so important to bring her to action?'

Troubridge's answer six hours later probably represents his actual reasons of the moment better than anything he later evolved, and is worthy of full quotation.

'With visibility at the time I could have been sighted from 20 to 25 miles away and could never have got nearer unless *Goeben* wished to bring me to action which she could have done under circumstances most advantageous to her. I could never have brought her to action. I had hoped to have engaged her at 3.30 in the morning in dim light but had gone north first with the object of engaging her in the entrance to the Adriatic.

'I was too late to intercept her when she altered course to the southward. In view of the immense importance of victory[3] or defeat at such an early stage of a war I would consider it a great imprudence to place squadron in such a position to be picked off at leisure and sunk while unable to effectively reply. The decision is not the easiest of the two to make I am well aware.'

Perhaps the most striking and, to later eyes, unconvincing argument here deployed is the idea that 'the immense importance of victory or defeat' at this stage of the conflict justified a bold engagement being dismissed as 'imprudent'.

But the countless other arguments must await a later chapter covering the massive official enquiries. For the moment we should return to the *Goeben*, still (as the Court Martial charge framed it) 'an enemy then flying'.

[3] This phrase was a sad—possibly conscious—echo of Admiral Sir John Jervis' remark shortly before the great battle in 1797 (whose name he was to bear as Lord St. Vincent): 'A victory is very necessary to England at this time'.

9

Towards the Golden Horn...and Beyond

'A little daring and a lot of luck.' SOUCHON

AS a result of Troubridge's decision, *Gloucester* was left 'in the forefront of the battle'. Milne remained at Malta, coaling his battle cruisers, until 8 August. *Gloucester*, small as she was, consumed coal at a rate of 350 tons a day, and by 7 August fuel was running short. Early that day she had been warned by Milne to drop gradually astern and avoid being captured. With Nelsonian enterprise Howard Kelly postponed any such negative action for eleven hours. Later he submitted in his report:

'As it was essential to know if the enemy were making for Egypt or for the Aegean Sea, it was considered permissible to continue shadowing.'

One must borrow Professor Marder's comprehensive tribute:

'Only the pertinacious and gallant Howard Kelly came out of the affair with honour and glory.'

Souchon was much farther ahead of his pursuers than he knew. Milne had been slow to get off the mark. But now fate intervened with a hideous blunder by Whitehall. At 2.30 pm on 8 August, while still some way short of Matapan, Milne received an Admiralty telegram: 'Commence hostilities at once against Austria.' In fact this telegram, anticipating the event by four days, was dispatched on the muddled initiative of a member of the Admiralty secretariat who saw the draft lying on a colleague's desk and sent it off. The outcome was as serious as even the enemy could have desired. Milne, with clear orders to do so, broke off the chase in *his* turn, and sailed north towards the Adriatic. By the time the mistake was recognized and put right, twenty-four hours had been wasted.

Souchon was still afraid to turn back to engage the *Gloucester*, even briefly, since he envisaged the battle cruisers coming up at any time at full speed over the horizon. However, a brief engagement did occur. Captain Howard Kelly tells of this action:

'At 1 pm, 7 August, when between Sapienza and Matapan, *Breslau* was dropping so far astern of *Goeben* that it was essential to make her close up or *Goeben* drop back, otherwise *Goeben* would soon have been out of sight. With this object in view, at 1.35 pm fire was opened with *Gloucester*'s fore 6-inch gun at a range of 11,500 yards at *Breslau*, then bearing two points on port bow of *Gloucester*. Breslau, having at the time her starboard guns bearing, replied at once with two ranging guns, and then went into salvo firing.'

Gloucester then increased to full speed and closed the range to about 10,000 yards (5 sea miles).

'The shooting of the *Breslau* was excellent, and a whole salvo of hers dropped along the line on the offside of *Gloucester*, none of them being more than 30 yards over. On fire being opened, the *Goeben* altered course 16 points to rejoin *Breslau* and opened fire but was far out of range ... *Gloucester* resumed her original course to follow the enemy, who were now close enough together to be kept in sight.

'On account of the service on which she was engaged, no effort was made by *Gloucester* to bring Breslau to close action; every effort on the contrary being devoted to maintaining all the faculties of *Gloucester* intact. Eighteen rounds of 6-inch were fired and fourteen rounds of 4-inch by *Gloucester*, and trustworthy reports were received later that *Breslau* had sustained damage in the action.'

After receiving this account the Admiralty (and it is now known that this was Churchill's own minute) informed Kelly:

'It is clear from a perusal of the report in question that the *Goeben* could have caught and sunk the *Gloucester* at any time had she dared to turn upon her. She was apparently deterred by the latter's boldness, which gave the impression of help close at hand. The combination of audacity with restraint, unswerving attention to the principal military object, viz, holding on to the *Goeben*, and strict conformity to orders, constitute a naval episode which may justly be regarded as a model.'

In two world wars, not many captains were to receive, from so hard a taskmaster, such unqualified praise.

An entertaining sidelight has been thrown on the later relationship between Howard Kelly and his brother Joe, whose ardent search for *Goeben* in the *Dublin* narrowly failed. They were both Irish eccentrics, and ended their respective careers as Admiral Sir Howard Kelly, Commander-in-Chief China, and Admiral of the Fleet Sir John Kelly, Commander-in-Chief Portsmouth. Between them there flourished a quarrel of longstanding and extreme vigour. In 1931 Sir Howard's yacht was wrecked on the pirate-ridden islands near Shanghai. By good fortune, no lives were lost. Sir John sent a cable: 'Glad you're safe.' The reply from Sir Howard read: 'Glad you're glad.'

One point relevant to Troubridge's inaction is of interest. *Gloucester*, with her relatively small guns (4-inch and 6-inch) hit the *Breslau* at 10,000 yards; Breslau's 4.1-inch guns also reached their target at this range; yet Troubridge repeatedly implied that his 9.2-inch guns were inaccurately calibrated beyond 8,000 yards.

That *Breslau* was hit is confirmed by Souchon.

'The *Breslau* received on her hull a shell which did her no harm. Although our ships had not exceeded a speed of 18 knots after the change of course, the English did not succeed in summoning other ships or destroyers to join them.

'We had shaken off the pursuit; but the enemy knew our position exactly, and our course and speed; the Dardanelles were still a long way off and we did not have enough coal to get there. Milne and Troubridge still had some good opportunities to overtake and fight us before we entered the Straits. I did not know where and at what distance from the *Gloucester* were the enemy forces. It was ahead of us that they were least likely to be. Also I thought that it was better to continue to advance in an easterly direction to make our pursuit more difficult.'

It was now mainly a question of staff work to find the collier he needed. They cruised among the Aegean isles, separately, avoiding the main shipping lanes. He could not make contact with Turkey by wireless, but used the liner, *General*, as a radio link. He told the German naval attaché at Constantinople:

' "Do the impossible so that I can pass through the Straits, with the permission of the Turkish Government, or even without their formal agreement." At dawn on 9 August, the *Goeben* anchored in the protected but remote bay of the rocky isle, Denusa [close to Naxos]. The *Breslau* rejoined her some hours later, followed by the collier.'

Both ships coaled simultaneously, one on each side, though at the same time cleared for action with steam up and ready to slip their anchor, while lookout-men on the tops of the isle swept the horizon continuously.

'We coaled the whole night. At dawn on 10 August, we sailed at 18 knots towards the Dardanelles. There was no sign of the enemy. And we heard no wireless messages which might enable us to judge if any enemy ship was near.'

However, though Souchon does not mention it, a vital signal was sent from Nauen, the German naval transmitter. Admiral Sir William James (in *The Eyes of the Navy*) tells us that this was one of the messages that were decyphered much later in Room 40:

'It is of the greatest importance to go to Constantinople as quickly as possible in order thereby to compel Turkey to side with us on the basis of the treaty that has been concluded. The Ambassador has been informed direct.'

Sir William adds a shrewd comment:

'If Fitzmaurice [the recalled diplomat] had warned our Government, or we had been able to decypher these signals, the destination of the *Goeben* and *Breslau* would have been gauged more accurately than was ever the case, and they might have been brought to action and never reached Constantinople, in which case Turkey might never have entered the war actively.'

Souchon was now on the threshold of triumph—though still lacking any accurate intelligence or direct radio help. He expected either to have to wait at the entrance to the Straits or even be compelled to force a passage. Luckily his ADC knew the position of the minefields, at least as they had been laid two years earlier. So they hoped to pass close to the shore on the European side.

'I decided to go ahead in spite of everything. The liner *General* wirelessed to us from Smyrna, but the message was mutilated: "Query entrance; demand surrender of forts." The rest indecypherable.'

Meanwhile, a considerable drama was being enacted on land. Enver, eager to assist, was still in trouble with his colleagues. Two members of the German Military Mission were with him, and one, Colonel von Kress, reported that the Turkish commander at Chanak in the Dardanelles was urgently requesting instruc-

7. Turkish sailors on the quarterdeck of *Yavuz*

8. *Yavuz*'s main (11-inch) and secondary (5.9-inch) armament

9. Admiral of the Fleet Sir John Kelly, drawn by Captain Jack Broome (at an earlier rank)

10. Enver Pasha, Turkish Minister for War, 1914

11. Troubridge with his Flag Captain, Fawcet Wray, on the quarterdeck of the Flagship

12. Winston Churchill, First Lord of the Admiralty, 1911 to 1915, with Admiral Prince Louis of Battenberg First Sea Lord, 1912 to 1914. (Photo taken in 1913)

tions. The two German ships were at the entrance to the Straits, seeking to enter. Enver said he must consult the Grand Vizier, but Kress pressed for an immediate answer. Enver sat silent for what seemed an endless period, then said abruptly, 'They are to be allowed to enter.'

'If the English warships follow them in are they to be fired on?' Again Enver hedged; he could not answer without consulting the Cabinet. But Kress kept up the pressure, and after another long pause, Enver said, 'Yes.'[1]

Souchon continues:

'At 16.00 hours we saw Tenedos and Imbros, the plain of Troy and the Hellespont. The entrance appeared free. With great anxiety and everyone at their battle posts ready to open fire, we entered the Narrows. I signalled by semaphore to Cape Helles: "Send a pilot at once." A Turkish destroyer approached us. He had a signal flying: "Follow me." I gave the hand of the Turkish Staff officer a friendly squeeze. He spoke German, and I had known him since my passage to Smyrna; I hugged our chief engineer, Breuer. Our ships anchored peacefully opposite Chanak before nightfall, and someone signalled that an enemy ship was coming towards the entrance.

'Our breakout had succeeded. Each man had done his duty. The reward was already a source of delight. The *Mittelmeer-Division* had broken the bonds which threatened us. We were ready for battle. The superior training of the Germans, a little daring and a lot of luck had resulted in a great military success. What the English had invited through their irresolution and the lack of initiative of their leaders was not slow to befall them.'

At first the ships remained at a temporary anchorage near Chanak well inside the Straits.

This was Wangenheim's moment of triumph. Glimpses of his delight have been recorded by the strongly pro-Allied American

[1] Barbara Tuchman, *August 1914.*

Ambassador. By a strange coincidence Morganthau was meeting his daughter off a small Italian ship, the *Sicilia*, at Constantinople on 10 August. 'The greeting proved even more interesting than I had expected.' The young lady had witnessed the brief encounter between the *Gloucester* and the German ships. This soon became known and both Wangenheim and the Austrian ambassador called at the American Embassy to interview this unexpected witness. What she had to tell them seemed to produce immense relief and satisfaction.

'They left the house in an almost jubilant mood, behaving as though a great weight had been taken off their minds. And certainly they had good reason for their elation.'

The next day Morganthau found his German colleague, for whom he had respect as a diplomat but sharp antipathy as a man, unduly preoccupied. Wangenheim kept looking out across the Bosphorus where he kept a small ship that acted as a wireless relay station. The American suggested that as something was clearly worrying his companion he should withdraw. 'No, no!' the Ambassador shouted. 'I want you to stay right where you are. This will be a great day for Germany!' Finally an envelope confirming the news arrived. 'We've got them ... The *Goeben* and the *Breslau* have passed through the Dardanelles.' The massive Wangenheim was waving the signal like a college boy. 'Of course you understand,' he added coyly, 'we have sold those ships to Turkey. And Admiral Souchon will enter the Sultan's service.' Morganthau at once realized that Wangenheim had 'clinched Turkey' as Germany's ally. 'All his intrigues and plottings for three years had now finally succeeded.' And he summed up the situation perceptively: 'I doubt if any two ships have exercised a greater influence upon history than these two German cruisers.'[2]

Wangenheim's diplomatic manoeuvres had been surprisingly sophisticated. He had won the public approval of the Turks. But the men in the know were not deceived. The Turks could not

[2] *Secrets of the Bosphorus.*

afford a realistic purchase price for the ships. But the farce was to be played out with gusto—to fool the general public. Souchon and his men sailed up the Bosphorus and anchored opposite the Russian Embassy. Officers and men lined the deck, solemnly removed the fezzes that they had acquired since arrival, put on German caps, sang German songs accompanied by the band, and, after an hour or two, replaced their original fezzes. The sale was a sham. The ships were not incorporated in the Turkish navy until after the war. The truth was, as Morganthau neatly expressed it, that the Turkish Navy was annexed to these German ships. And, apart from receiving a handful of Turkish sailors for the sake of appearances, the German crews under German officers remained in active charge.

It was at this time that Djavid, the peace-loving Minister of Finance, met a distinguished Belgian and told him that the Germans had captured Brussels. The Belgian retorted, pointing to the *Goeben* lying at anchor, 'I have even more terrible news for you. The Germans have captured Turkey.'

Souchon, who may well have recalled Napoleon's dictum that you can do anything with bayonets except sit on them, had no intention of accepting a static role. And the situation continued to develop in his favour. On 16 August there was a solemn ceremony near the Golden Horn. The Turkish Naval Minister officially received the two ships into the Ottoman navy, and *Goeben* and *Breslau* were now rechristened *Yavuz Sultan Selim* and *Midilli*. The farce had become a national drama.

It seems almost ironic that early in September Troubridge was appointed Senior Naval Officer, Dardanelles. It was in this temporary but important command, with a major force at his disposal, that he received the following signal from Churchill:

'8 September, 1914, 5.45 pm.

Your sole duty is to sink the *Goeben* and *Breslau*, under whatever flag, if they come out of the Dardanelles. The safety of important convoys of troops from Egypt and other issues of the highest importance depend on your doing this. For this purpose you should use and dispose your whole force including the submarines, when they arrive, and the destroyers. Enemy must be destroyed at all costs by night or day.'[3]

This splendidly bellicose order was, alas, of little use. Souchon had no intention of emerging to face certain destruction.

As the end of October approached Turkey had still not declared war; though Morganthau detected a sinister mood. There were regular evening parties on the *General*, the liner that had so faithfully supported and followed the *Goeben*. Tongues were loosened by ample supplies of beer and champagne and on all sides bellicose assertions could be heard. If Turkey did not act, they said, then the Germans would provoke Russia and implicate the Turks. Morganthau found the German officers 'just like a lot of boys with chips on their shoulders'. (The phrase sounds anachronistic, but it was current in the USA from about 1880, though slow to reach the UK. They were 'simply spoiling for a fight . . . impetuous and *'kriegslustig'*—eager for war.

Behind the scenes there was much activity—especially by the sabre-rattling Enver. At an earlier stage, he had authorised Souchon to take his ships into the Black Sea and attack any Russian ships he might encounter. The Cabinet, however, overruled this aggressive plan. Souchon, angry and frustrated, protested passionately against the Turkish vacillation. Wangenheim supported the admiral and insisted that, though the ships might fly the Ottoman flag, they had not relinquished their German character; and in any case, to Germans inactivity was 'shameful'. In the middle of much havering and many reversals of policy, the Turkish Government expressed a wish to appoint Souchon formally as Vice-Admiral in the Ottoman naval service for a year. Late in September Souchon went through the reassuring motion of a solemn promise not to involve any Turkish ships in belligerent acts without prior authority. It was not a promise that he seemed likely to keep, or in fact was slow to break. Two days

[3] Lumby.

later Enver personally ordered the still operative navigation channel through the Dardanelles to be sealed off. Surprisingly this was done without collusion with the Germans.

The shaky finances of the Turks required help from Berlin and in early October a trainload of 1 million Turkish pounds in gold was passed through Rumania and reached Constantinople in four days—a near record for speed, it was claimed. Soon another consignment arrived safely, and now Enver felt no further obstacles in his path. Full intervention was almost under way.

All kinds of devious schemes were devised by Enver and the German Foreign Office and High Command to precipitate war. Enver fancied an arrangement whereby he would supply Souchon with sealed orders, and then signal to him *not* to open them. This would put the onus on the admiral to manufacture his own 'incident'. Even Wangenheim drew the line at this perversion of diplomacy. By 25 October, orders were clarified a little further. Souchon was to take 'the entire fleet' and seek a suitable opportunity to attack the Russian fleet. The Turkish Minister of Marine sent secret instructions to his own senior officers on board

to comply with Souchon's orders. The fleet sailed on 27 October, ostensibly on manoeuvres. Souchon decided to go far beyond his orders; he would not wait on a chance encounter with the Russian fleet—he would deliberately bombard coastal installations. This would be a provocation that none could dispute, and it made war not probable but certain. Two days later the irrevocable act was committed. Odessa, Sevastopol and Novorossisk were shelled, mines were laid in shipping lanes and a few Russian ships were destroyed. Souchon boldly reported that, in response to what he called Russian interference, 'hostilities have been opened today' and Wangenheim delightedly sent an immediate message to this effect to Berlin.

Just as the arrival of the German ships had initially caused alarm in the capital, so this *fait accompli* provoked a cabinet crisis. The Grand Vizier protested that he had not been consulted and insisted that all operations be suspended. Enver obliged outwardly and ordered the fleet to cease fire, but added a 'hint' to Souchon to turn a blind eye. It was not so much Machiavellian as unnecessary. The Grand Vizier and four other ministers declared their intention to resign. But again Enver promised to send a note of conciliation to Petrograd, Paris and London. However, conciliation was rightly viewed as a sham, when the false excuse of Russian provocation was made. The Grand Vizier's attempts to dissociate himself were crushed by Talaat's reminder that he had signed the Alliance of 2 August with Germany. But it was the implied threat to his life rather than Talaat's forceful arguments that persuaded him not to resign. In Turkey a threat of this kind was far from idle. The life of an Ottoman politician was apt to be nasty, brutish and short. The aphorism is in this context severely factual, for the Grand Vizier and the Ministers for the Interior and of Marine—Said Halim, Talaat and Djemal—were all assassinated shortly after the war; Djavid, the comparatively pacific Minister of Finance, was hanged in 1926 for conspiring to assassinate Mustapha Kemal—at best a desperate undertaking; and Enver (whose courage, though not his honesty, was never in doubt) died in

1922 leading a forlorn hope—a cavalry charge in Turkestan against the Bolsheviks.

Four days after Souchon's attack on Russian ports, the Tsarist Government declared war on the Ottoman empire—and Souchon's ambitious and improbable task had been fulfilled.

The British hoped to prevent open war by a sharp demonstration of seapower. Admiral Carden, lately in charge of the dockyard at Malta, and now replacing Milne and Troubridge, was ordered to undertake a curious sort of punitive or deterrent operation. The Admiralty signal ran:

'1 November, 1914, 9.45 pm: Urgent. Without risking ships a demonstration is to be made by bombardment on the earliest suitable day by your armoured ships and the two French battleships against the Forts at the entrance of the Dardanelles at a range of 14,000 to 12,000 yards.'

In due course Carden reported that he had carried out orders:

'The object aimed at was to do as much damage as possible in a short time with a limited number of rounds at long range, and to turn away before the fire from the forts became effective. Eight rounds per turret were allowed.'

Thus, contrary to what is commonly believed, the first bombardment of the Dardanelles was carried out, not in February, 1915, but three months previously. Fort Sedd-el-Bahr, on the tip of the Gallipoli peninsula, was reduced to ruins, and Carden could report that Turco-German casualties were at least 150. The bombardment, however, failed to break Turkish resolution, and may have had precisely the reverse effect. Jellicoe wrote after the war that it was an 'unforgiveable error'. So two days later Britain and France, left with no alternative, declared war on Turkey. In Churchill's characteristic phrase, 'the curse descended irrevocably'.

There remained one final humiliation in March, 1915—the ultimate naval and diplomatic rebuff. Hearing that his Director of Naval Intelligence was negotiating to buy Turkish neutrality,

Lord Fisher intervened. He cancelled the negotiations and ordered a fresh approach. Britain would make a bid to buy the *Goeben* for £200,000 and the *Breslau* for half this princely sum.

But the Turks, whose ownership was, in any case, purely notional, were not interested—and the misguided affair ground to an inevitable standstill.

10

A Scurry of Scapegoats

'It was necessary that someone should suffer for the escape of the Goeben.*'* TROUBRIDGE

THE chilling shock of the *Goeben*'s escape was at first diminished by the general misjudgement of its character and consequences. Corbett contrasts the shadow, later cast by this 'unhappy affair', with the

> 'burst of public derision that the Germans should so soon have been chased out of the Mediterranean to suffer an ignominious internment ... It was many months before it was possible to appreciate fully the combined effrontery, promptitude and sagacity of the move.'

The Prime Minister recorded in his diary that the first news was 'interesting'—adding in a vein that was part of his magisterial approach, that 'we shall insist' on displacing the German crews, so 'it does not much matter'. But by November even Asquith's complacency had been sufficiently shaken for him to report formally to the King, that

> 'the Cabinet were of opinion that ... the escape of the *Goeben* ... is not creditable to the officers of the Navy.'

History does not relate whether this critical comment was seen by the First Lord—most probably not.

One of the most astonishing aspects of the *Goeben*'s escape is the complete absence from the Royal Archives of any letters concerning the episode. It is well known that George V took an exceptionally close professional interest in all Navy matters. There are many long letters, some couched in tones of angry protest, addressed to Churchill as First Lord, dealing with such controversial questions as fresh names for new ships in the rapidly expanding pre-war Navy. The King was also accustomed to receive unsolicited and very frank comments from old service friends such as Admiral Sir Stanley Colville. Some idea of the freedom extended to an old shipmate may be gathered from the candour of a letter on the occasion of Churchill's dismissal from the Admiralty in May, 1915. Colville wrote to the King: 'he was, we all consider, a danger to the Empire'.

The two very senior admirals, Sir George Callaghan and Sir Hedworth Meux, who sat on the preliminary Court of Enquiry, were on close terms with their Sovereign : the first was a Knight Grand Cross of the Royal Victorian Order, and the other a Knight Commander of the Royal Victorian Order—honours which indicate personal services. Milne himself, also a GCVO, felt deeply aggrieved at being deprived of a promised senior appointment as Commander-in-Chief the Nore, and it would have seemed certain that he would wish to lay his case before the King. The total absence of any apologia, any enquiry by the King, or any comment submitted to him, is remarkable. One senses that all concerned were so uneasy at this miserable performance that silence was the only fitting response.

But it was not long before the Admiralty, and indeed the Navy as a whole, were anxiously looking around for a scapegoat. Clearly *someone* had blundered, and it was natural if possible to identify the culprit. Ultimately the role of chief suspect was thrust on Admiral Troubridge, the second-in-command. The details, first of a Court of Enquiry, and then of a Court Martial before five admirals and four captains, give the best guide as to whether the allegation of negligence was fair.

There were other protagonists who were anxious about their reputations. And over the years lengthy *pièces justificatives* appeared. These are worth a little study before we return to the legal battles that erupted around Troubridge.

Four men felt the need to leave written accounts justifying their accounts. Troubridge's Flag Captain, Fawcet Wray, had enjoyed a highly successful earlier career. He had served as staff commander to Lord Charles Beresford, the Commander-in-Chief, Mediterranean, flying his flag in the battleship *King Edward VII*. In a photograph of 'Charlie B.' with his staff, Wray looks the ideal type of rising young officer, handsome and dedicated. But it was not wholly an advantage to have been favoured by Beresford. At this time his Chief of Staff was Sturdee; and even this enviable post was later considered a barrier to further promotion, with Fisher again in charge at the Admiralty. It may be that the harsh treatment accorded to Wray in some measure reflects the hostility of Fisher; for he had been brought back as First Sea Lord on 30 October during the post-mortem on the *Goeben* affair. Wray now found himself 'virtually ostracized' by his brother officers; furthermore Churchill refused to see him and hear his evidence at first hand. Stung by the injustice of this embargo, and of not being allowed to make a statement to clear himself at the Court Martial, he felt it was a 'matter of justice to my personal and professional reputation and honour' to make a written sworn Declaration in August, 1917. This statement began by referring to allegations of 'cowardice and default'. He then summarized his case: that it was his duty to tender advice to Troubridge at 3.30 am on 7 August; that he did not intend to dissuade his Admiral from continuing the chase of the *Goeben*; and that when he found that the chase was being abandoned he remonstrated with Troubridge. He knew that the Rear-Admiral 'had orders not to get engaged with a superior force'; also that outside 16,000 yards 'the *Goeben* was an infinitely superior force to the First Cruiser Squadron'. What Wray proposed was to await the *Goeben* in the Straits of Otranto, and to drive her towards either shore and thus get within range of the Squadron's guns. This proposal Troubridge did not accept. After they had turned to steam

95

south, Wray went to Troubridge at 2.45 am, forty-five minutes earlier than the final conversation, to ask, 'Are you going to fight?' Wray admitted that later he realized his advice to 'lie across the *Goeben*'s bows and more or less go bald-headed for her' was too hasty. During the short interval he became convinced that Goeben would spot them at 25 to 30 miles, and either steam round them or, by engaging outside 16,000 yards 'she could pick us off one at a time'. He evidently had no inkling of the tactical opportunities for attacking with four cruisers; he could not anticipate—and it would be less than fair to expect—what Commodore Harwood achieved so brilliantly a quarter of a century later at the Battle of the River Plate. He assumed, he says, that *Goeben* was a 27-knot ship, though with her long absence from a dry dock this was from his viewpoint a distinctly flattering opinion. So he returned half an hour later to explain his revised thoughts. He now believed that the proposed action should be reconsidered.

'I did not go to him to advise him to abandon the chase. I admit that at this period I had no other plan to suggest. [When Troubridge gave orders to alter course towards the East, Wray thought he was merely hauling off to gain time while he asked the C-in-C for instructions, and also to reconsider the problem.] I frankly admit I was astonished when he announced his intention to the Squadron of abandoning the chase.'

Wray conceded that what Troubridge said at his Court Martial cleared him, but Wray was upset because 'owing to his attitude towards me since the Court Martial the effect of it has been nullified'. Troubridge had apparently tried to persuade Wray not to take any action on his own to clear his honour. In January, 1915, Troubridge had promised to make a point of clearing Wray's conduct with Churchill. But two weeks later Wray received a dusty answer. No, Troubridge told him, he had not spoken to the First Lord, and didn't see why he should, because 'after all if it had not been for me (Wray), he would have fought the *Goeben*'. This did not seem to square with what

Troubridge had told the Court, and Wray said as much. But the gulf of fixed disagreement between these two men had deepened, and Troubridge then told him:

> 'My dear Wray, by the time you are an Admiral and have a staff of your own, you will realize that you must be loyal to your Staff. *I did that to save you.*' (Wray's italics.)

Wray wound up his long declaration with a reminder that Milne and Troubridge had both been cleared, while he had been deprived of any chance to clear his honour.[1]

It is not related to whom this formal declaration was sent; at all events Wray was left with his grievance. In fact, he had already been appointed to command the *Talbot* at Gallipoli where he won the DSO. He was promoted Rear-Admiral on retirement in 1922, and finished up, as was the happy custom of those spacious days, as a Vice-Admiral.

The next apologia came in peculiar circumstances from Milne. Sir Julian Corbett had published the first volume of his authoritative *Naval Operations* in 1920. Much that Corbett knew could not then be fully revealed. But the title page bore the sub-heading 'History of the Great War—based on official documents'. And Corbett, though a very balanced and restrained historian, had felt bound to make some critical comments on Milne's activities—or inactivity. The most important issue raised by Corbett concerned Milne's dispositions once he knew at 5 am on 5 August that both German ships were probably back at Messina. He might well have played safe by guarding both outlets from Messina, outside territorial waters, using all three battle cruisers. This would have forced Souchon's hand, with no choice but to fight heavier ships or face internment, as to which the Italians had already given warning.

Milne's apologia at this point becomes almost inarticulate; to think that a mere landsman like Corbett (who was in fact widely regarded as the leading authority on naval history) should offer any criticism of *him*, the senior admiral on the spot.

[1] Lumby.

Another issue was Milne's failure to send the *Indomitable* in pursuit on 7 August while the other two battle cruisers were coaling. (*Indomitable* had already coaled at Bizerta.) Milne was at pains—and his prose was as laboured as his tactical thought— to explain that this ship had boiler defects, and that, had she chased the *Goeben*, she would have run out of coal at the critical moment when war with Austria was announced. However, Milne, whose reasoning is unimpressive, was factually incorrect about the fuel situation. Captain Creswell, who dealt with these operations when on the directing staff of the RN College in 1932, examined the facts and found that all three ships could have steamed at 22 knots to the eastern limits of the Mediterranean and returned to Malta without difficulty; and he concluded that if only Milne had followed up hard he would have been only a few hours astern. Milne's limited and rigid outlook did not allow him to look beyond the difficulties. And, as Creswell has put it, 'You will never catch a ship if you don't chase her.'

Milne would never have understood Wellington's simple explanation of his first victory: 'When one is strongly intent on an object, common sense will usually direct one to the right means.'

But there is no need to spend any more time on Milne's essay in rehabilitation. One is left, after a study of his book, with the sad impression of an ungenerous and petty personality and a shallow mind. This was a Commander-in-Chief whom Churchill might wisely have passed over—as Fisher had argued so fiercely two years earlier. In the event he was denied the Nore Command, which (as Fisher put it) should be kept for Jellicoe 'when he comes back with one arm'. In fact the Nore Command went to Callaghan.

Apart from his 1921 book, Milne's subsequent pursuit of a martyr's crown makes strange reading. The papers that he left contain a mass of memoranda, letters—drafted and received— and of official records. As a commentary by Milne on Milne it is a revealing set of documents. Much of the contentious correspondence took place five or six years after the events in question. In 1916 he had written to Admiral Colville, irritated that, while he (Milne) was on half-pay, Troubridge was winning laurels in Serbia. Colville's reply is adroit:

'If you will allow me to say so, I do not quite see your point that Troubridge's appointment, lent to a Foreign power for duty *on shore*, bears any weight; if he had hoisted his flag as an Admiral RN it would have been very different.'[2]

Soon after Jutland a letter to Milne from the Editor of the *Daily Express* shows by implication how agitated he had become even with people outside the service: 'This damned human factor, even among admirals, takes all the fineness out of things.'

Churchill's letters strike a distinctly cool note—and we can guess that Fisher, who had been so acid in his comments when Milne was appointed in 1912, would hardly abstain from saying 'I told you so'.

In 1919 the borbardment of Their Lordships had lasted for five years, and the Secretary, Sir Oswyn Murray, had had enough. He referred to Milne's request—whether intended seriously or merely as a gesture—for a Court Martial, and ended: 'I am to add that Their Lordships are not prepared to accede to your request to be tried by Court Martial.' This would seem enough finally to close the matter, but a year later, furious at Corbett's mild criticisms, Milne consulted his solicitors as to some legal remedy against Corbett or his sponsors, the Admiralty. They advised against any action, which would (they said) at best be very costly.

But Milne had not finished, and his mounting sense of injustice reached an almost paranoid pitch. Letters to Jellicoe, to Beatty, to Balfour and many others were sent, and their cautious or indifferent replies carefully kept—as evidence of a pitiable obsession.

The next major contribution came from the pen of Winston Churchill. Writing in 1923, he had access to many but not all of

[2] Milne Papers.

the relevant signals, documents, and books, including those by Milne and Corbett. He was greatly concerned about the *Goeben*'s escape. As Barbara Tuchman says, Churchill set out

'to compose a narrative that, while not too obviously blaming the naval commanders, would show the Admiralty to have been blameless and still claim to be history, not special pleading. This delicate feat of balancing was accomplished by placing the blame for failure to arrest the *Goeben* on accidents of fate ... The account is one to be read with caution not incompatible with admiration.'

Churchill naturally picks on Milne's failure to block *both* entrances to the Straits of Messina. And he is critical of the *Indomitable* being sent to coal at Bizerta (which took an unduly long time) when instant facilities were available at Malta, where she would have been well placed to close the southern exit. Churchill then considers the failure of the Admiralty to authorize our ships to follow *Goeben* into the Straits on 6 August.

'Had it been put to me I should at once have consented. This was no petty incident and the prize was well worth the risk of vexing the Italians.'

But neither Prince Louis nor Sturdee suggested it.

He strongly upholds the signal of 30 July which referred to the need to 'avoid action with superior forces'. Though this has since become notorious for its ambiguity, he makes, as would be expected, a spirited defence. Without actually disclosing that it was drafted, as we now know, in his own hand, he justifies it as a model of clarity.

The exciting tale, as seen through the First Lord's eyes, is brought vividly to life. One cannot fail to share the sheer physical exitement building up in the silent rooms of the Admiralty during a naval confrontation. But there is a subtle emphasis on fate; and in the following famous passage Churchill develops his theme:

'In all this story of the escape of the *Goeben* one seems to see the influence of that sinister fatality which at a later stage and on a far larger scale was to dog the enterprise against the Dardanelles. The terrible "If's" accumulate. If my first thoughts on 27 July of sending the *New Zealand* to the Mediterranean had materialized; if we could have opened fire on the *Goeben* during the afternoon of 4 August; if we had been less solicitous for Italian neutrality; if Sir Berkeley Milne had sent the *Indomitable* to coal at Malta instead of Bizerta; if the Admiralty had sent him direct instructions when on the night of the 5th they learned where the *Goeben* was; if Rear-Admiral Troubridge in the small hours of 7 August had not changed his mind; if the *Dublin* and her two destroyers had intercepted the enemy during the night of the 6th–7th—the story of the *Goeben* would have ended here.'

A little while after the publication of the first volume of *The World Crisis*, Troubridge put in writing his long-considered thoughts on the most critical week of his career. This paper he called a 'Rough Account of *Goeben* and *Breslau*'. He is quick to point out important precedents for the Commander-in-Chief being court-martialled if his second-in-command was acquitted. He even asserts that Milne should himself have applied for a Court Martial, a suggestion which, with our knowledge of that evasive personality, might raise a smile. However, as we have seen, this he eventually did, though in different circumstances, in 1919.

But his main target is Churchill, whose Private Secretary and Chief of Staff he had been, and into whose complex nature he had considerable insight. And it is on Churchill's *The World Crisis* that he fastens.

'Mr Churchill has . . . written a book. Mr Churchill is a politician and though his book is a genuine attempt to write history, it is, subconsciously perhaps, coloured by a desire to prove that his administration was without fault.'

This was a palpable hit. He continues with a complaint about the 'complete detachment of the Admiralty from the affair'. Then, in a disarming passage, he speaks of his late master in unusual terms :

'I have a great respect and esteem for Mr Churchill. He induces an almost motherly affection in officers who serve him, as he himself has so much of the child in his character.'

Troubridge shows his resentment at Churchill's statement that

'he cannot understand why Admiral Troubridge "changed his mind"—but I never changed my mind; as I propose to relate, a line of conduct relative to the *Goeben* had been laid down by me *ab initio* and from that I never changed. How often Mr Churchill has said to me, "In politics one can never afford to admit that one has made a mistake." And so he remains true to principle in his book.'

The *Rough Account* goes on to emphasize that Milne was later quite unable to suggest any method by which a slow squadron in the open sea can close a fast battle cruiser. And he scores a further point by stressing that a First Lord, with a hundred other questions coming to him daily, is perhaps in a less good position to judge a squadron's fighting capacity than the admiral who had been in command for eighteen months. He did not need to shelter behind the instruction to avoid a superior force. 'It was a principle I should in any case have followed.' Troubridge explained that his staff had calculated that even if the *Goeben* sighted the squadron when they were dead ahead, she could steam round them at 16,000 yards, outside their range, in seventy-two minutes.

But this was surely a counsel of defeat. No one could have blamed the admiral if this had happened, and nothing damaging would have befallen his squadron. Angered by Churchill's question, 'Why did he change his mind?' Troubridge raises a fresh point: that it was worthwhile to steam on, in case dull weather with poor visibility gave them a better chance to close.

In the event the weather at 3.30 am was perfect—'all objects visible at almost any distance'. So he gave the order to turn on to a course parallel to the *Goeben*'s, 40 miles on her port bow. A signal to Milne at 4 am reporting the provisional decision gave him a chance to order battle at all costs. No reply came for six hours. For this 'no real explanation was ever given'.

Troubridge then comes to the interview he had had with Milne before leaving Malta. Milne invited his second-in-command to go fully into every detail, to criticize his written orders freely, and ask any questions about them. So once again the ambiguous Admiralty instruction about superior forces was bandied around, with Milne conceding that Troubridge as the man on the spot must be the final arbiter. But at that stage Milne had told Troubridge that, on orders just received from London, he would have two battle cruisers added to his force. As we have seen these were withdrawn on 3 August, also on Admiralty orders.

A final accusation in the *Rough Account* is important.

'Captain Vere, one of Armstrong Vickers' representatives, actually told the Embassy before war was declared that Constantinople was the destination of the *Goeben*. He told me this personally ... adding that his information came straight from the Turkish Minister of Marine, and he thought it his duty to communicate it to the Embassy at once. He was told to go about his business.

The whole course of the affair would have been changed had the Embassy communicated this important item of news to England.'

Before appearing at the Court of Enquiry, Troubridge was told by the Naval Secretary, Admiral Hood, that the enquiry was general and not into *his* conduct. This was later contradicted, but it left Troubridge with the impression that, there being no charge against him, he was under no obligation to say anything. However, he decided to speak—only to find that Milne's recollection of the crucial interview did not at all agree with his.

After recapitulating some of the expert evidence, Troubridge adds with understandable bitterness:

'It was necessary that someone should suffer for the escape of the *Goeben*. The First Lord of the Admiralty certainly was not going to accept any blame. The First Sea Lord, Prince Louis of Battenberg, neither, while as I have above related the C-in-C was not prepared to shoulder any responsibility. There only remained myself.'

The ultimate scapegoat had been isolated—and, after the preliminary Enquiry, there followed the almost unparalleled humiliation for a flag officer of being court-martialled for negligence.

At this point we may glance briefly forward to see how both admirals fared. Unlike Milne, who was left on half pay for the rest of the war, Troubridge was given a rather unusual role—entirely remote from the service at sea to which his whole being was devoted. In January, 1915, he was sent to Serbia, herself the original victim of Austrian aggression, where he headed a British Naval Mission, to help with the evacuation of soldiers and refugees. In Newbolt's words,

'his influence with the Serbian generals was very great. From the moment he arrived on the Danube he won their affection and respect. Throughout the retreat his proud military bearing and the self-control of his officers had been noticed by everybody. The Serbian authorities were very bitter about the Allies; but their affection for the British admiral had never wavered, and when they arrived at the coast one of their first acts had been to give him authority over their own soldiers and fellow countrymen.'[3]

At one stage Troubridge found it necessary to insist on a change on the Serbian plans for evacuation. His firmness was readily accepted, and an engaging letter from the Serbian GHQ, couched in slightly Balkan English, reached him:

[3] *Naval Operations*, Vol. IV.

'We consider you our greatest friend and we are happy to have so competent and illustrious an officer for our naval affairs. We shall always address ourselves to you, and your advice will always be held most precious.'

During the following year he was given command of a naval contingent; in this post he was 'successful in preventing Belgrade from being bombarded and the Serbian troops harassed'. By 1919 his exceptional services had been honoured with a knighthood—(he was not in direct line for his father's baronetcy which passed later to his grandson), and he was promoted full admiral. His *Rough Account*, which was written only about a year before his death in 1926, was not published until 1970.

This document, written by hand in an ordinary notebook, cannot conceal his inevitable bitterness towards some of those who placed massive responsibilties on his shoulders, and then left him, unsupported, in the forefront of the verbal battle. Nevertheless he was everywhere held in high regard; and one who had been 'the handsomest officer in the Navy in his younger days' left behind him the memory of a most attractive personality. And he left, too, a worthy heir. Vice-Admiral Sir Thomas Troubridge, who commanded a large section of the naval force at the Sicily landings in 1943, was his only son. There is high authority for believing that only his early death prevented his rise 'to the highest posts which the Royal Navy can offer'.

11

Recall and Inquisition

'A danger to the State.' BATTENBERG ON TROUBRIDGE

SO much for the later efforts at exculpation by these four
protagonists. It is time now to return to Troubridge himself
and trace events as they affected him. The Furies, he must have
felt, were closing in on him.

On 16 August, while still at sea in *Defence*, Troubridge made
the customary routine report to Milne—but this was to prove
very much more than a formality. He retraced the steps he had
taken up to 11 August, with which we are now familiar. By then
he knew that the Germans were safely ensconced in the Marmora.
He resumed his patrol at the mouth of the Adriatic, and two
days later was ordered to commence hostilities with Austria. On
the 15th he made a rendezvous with the French Fleet. Later he
shifted his flag to *Indefatigable*, and maintained a watch at the
entrance to the Dardanelles. On 25 August, while still at sea, he
was told to amplify the reasons governing his action on 7 August:
in plain terms, to explain why he abandoned the chase at dawn.

A number of points were now brought out for the first time.
These can be briefly summarized: Troubridge had felt himself
bound to husband his forces especially at this early stage in the
war; he held that 'the multiplication of cruisers' had no bearing
on whether or not to engage the enemy in the open sea; he believed that his squadron's speed in company was limited to 17
knots; they had never registered hits at over 8,000 yards, due to
the large spread of the guns; he was very sure, initially, that

Goeben was bound for the Adriatic, since it then seemed futile for her to proceed to the eastern Mediterranean; he still hoped that the battle cruisers would be returned to his command. He then dealt with the hopeless prospect, as he saw it, of attempting to engage this powerful enemy unit. 'I was therefore placed in a cruel position.' Though his squadron were eager to fight and ready under any circumstances, he saw the *Goeben* as the superior force that he was not to engage.

'All I could gain would be the reputation of having attempted something which, though predestined to be ineffective, would be indicative of the boldness of our spirit. I felt that more than that was expected of an Admiral entrusted by Their Lordships with great responsibilities.'

He looked with contempt on any senior officer who acted for his own immediate interests. He had had the full support of his squadron captains in avoiding action. Had he acted otherwise, he

'would have subjected the Squadron to almost certain defeat, if not disaster, and not been worthy of the trust reposed in a flag officer to sink his personal considerations in great emergencies, with a single view to the ultimate advantage of our arms.

'I trust their Lordships will consider my action to be worthy of their support and approval.'[1]

This the Admiralty were very far from doing. Prince Louis wrote a minute the next day which was sharply hostile to Troubridge. Milne's account was received with qualified approval. But the First Sea Lord was clearly angered at what had emerged regarding Troubridge. He had, wrote Battenberg, 'signally failed in carrying out the task assigned to him'. His first message to Milne, telling of his decision to break off the chase, was dismissed by Prince Louis as 'his subordinate's amazing telegram'. It was hard to imagine that the risks readily accepted by the little

[1] Lumby.

Gloucester were less than for the four larger cruisers. But he still categorized the *Goeben* as 'a harmless fugitive'. Below this long minute, is a very brief footnote by the First Lord: 'The explanation is satisfactory, the result unsatisfactory. (signed) W.S.C.'

Worse was to follow: eleven days later Battenberg wrote a further minute specifically on Troubridge's report. Part of this formidable indictment runs thus:

> 'Admiral Troubridge states that with four armoured cruisers he could never bring to action in daylight the German battle cruiser *Goeben*. He consequently failed to carry out his clear duty, both tactically in declining to attack the enemy, and strategically in not heading off the enemy (for which he was very favourably placed) and driving him back into the arms of the superior force under the C.-in-C.'[2]

The minute then deals with the armament of the opposed forces —particularly the contrast between twenty-two British 9.2-inch guns and ten German 11-inch guns. He refers to the designed speeds as 23 knots (*Defence*) and 27 knots (*Goeben*). 'Not one of the excuses which Admiral Troubridge gives can be accepted for one moment.' The effective gun range, in Battenberg's view, did not differ greatly. The German single target was much larger than the four separate British targets. 'Superior speed (which undoubtedly existed) in a single ship can be nullified by *proper tactical dispositions of four units*.' (Author's italics.)

So there were some senior officers who fully recognized that four ships, skilfully handled, could impose very awkward problems for a single larger ship.

> 'The escape of the *Goeben* must ever remain a shameful episode in this war. The flag officer who is responsible for this failure cannot be entrusted with any further command afloat and his continuance in such command constitutes a danger to the State.

2 Lumby.

'I therefore propose that Rear-Admiral Troubridge be directed to return to England forthwith.'

The degree of Battenberg's hostility—not to say venom—is disclosed in a letter written on 27 August, 1914 (before any formal enquiry) to Milne:

'Secret. It is with great satisfaction that our official letter [exonerating Milne] is now going to you, which expresses full approval of all you have done. Having no inkling of Troubridge's amazing misconduct, the whole situation was wrapt in mystery. The slowness of our ships is disgusting and must have been exasperating to you in your difficult situation.

'I trust you understand that in not seeing you the other day I was bound by a Board decision. Looking forward to seeing you tomorrow,

I am,

Yours as ever,

Louis Battenberg.'[3]

This was special pleading with a vengeance, and one wonders if it crossed Prince Louis' charitable mind that the 'disgusting slowness' might include the responses of the Commander-in-Chief.

Battenberg's indictment closed with the order that Admiral Sir Hedworth Meux, Commander-in-Chief Portsmouth, should be directed to hold a Court of Enquiry with Sir George Callaghan (who had just been relieved as Commander-in-Chief, Grand Fleet, by Jellicoe); Milne was to attend as a witness. Prince Louis had not yet seen Troubridge's second disclaimer, but when it arrived he added simply that no new factors were disclosed by it. All these arrangements were endorsed by Churchill.

Thus began the two formidable trials of a luckless admiral. The preliminary Court of Enquiry packed into a single day a vast amount of evidence. In fact most of the evidence was heard from

[3] Milne Papers.

2.30 pm onwards. This was possible only on account of a minimum of cross-examination.

In the Navigation School, Portsmouth, the legal sighting shots were quickly fired. Milne was called first. He covered ground that it would be tedious to go over again; but he made the reasonable point which Battenberg had pressed, that it would be difficult for the *Goeben* to engage four ships at once, since everyone knew that one ship found it as much as she could do to exercise effective gunnery control against even two ships.

It also emerged that, coal shortages apart, Troubridge had eight destroyers with him, and he was counting on being reinforced by the light cruiser *Dublin* and two more destroyers.

Troubridge then embarked on a long and presumably closely prepared statement. He began with three special points : that all his signals and reports had been governed by a determination not to criticise Milne or *his* actions, or indulge in reproaches or recriminations; that the Admiralty were morally bound to support a squadron commander who, in obeying their directions, took a decision likely to damage his reputation. Thirdly he insisted that only the admiral 'who is in the face of the enemy' could gauge what precise combination of ships, in the conditions prevailing at that moment, were to be judged a superior force.

He then explained that in pre-war manoeuvres, in an encounter with the battle cruiser, *Lion*, at long range, his ship was judged by the Chief Umpire to be disabled. (It seems to have been overlooked that *Lion's* guns were 13.5-inch not 11-inch.) 'I came away with the fixed and unalterable opinion that the advent of battle cruisers had killed the armoured cruiser.' He told Milne in 1913 of this view, and was asked by him to lecture on this to all the officers of the Mediterranean Fleet.

As he ranged over the evidence he recalled Nelson's records of terrible uncertainties and endless surmises. These of course were concerned with where the enemy was aiming, not whether to seek action—a problem that surely seldom crossed Nelson's mind. There is a single reference to his belief that the British 9.2-inch shells would not penetrate the *Goeben*'s armour. (This was over 10 inches thick, maximum, at the waterline belt.)

Occasionally the Court interposed a question, such as: 'You would hardly expect the *Goeben* to sink your four cruisers in that easy manner, would you?' And again the rather pointed comment: 'It seems to me that you are assuming the *Goeben* has everything perfect and that your own (squadron) is rather bad.' And the Court emphasized that Troubridge did have command of four cruisers, not one.

At last the torrent of words on that tense afternoon came to an end, and the next day the two Admirals forwarded their official conclusions. Troubridge, they found, had long been obsessed with his opinion that the *Goeben* was superior to 'any number of non-battle-cruisers'. The Court stated that the British weight of broadside per minute (for the armoured cruisers would have a faster rate of fire) was superior to the *Goeben*'s. But they conceded that *Goeben* had much greater speed and heavier armour. They contended that the opinion of Troubridge and Wray about the *Goeben*'s superlative shooting was not founded on precise and positive evidence. The Squadron (with aid from *Gloucester, Dublin*, and the two destroyers *Beagle* and *Bulldog*) 'had a very fair chance of at least delaying *Goeben* by materially damaging her'. And they regretted that the Rear-Admiral had not beforehand made it clear to Milne 'that he had no intention to engage *Goeben* in open water in daylight with his Squadron unless supported by a battle cruiser.'[4]

The curtain-raiser was over. The main drama was announced to the Accused (as he was now officially designated) in these terms:

> 'Sir, I am to acquaint you that having carefully considered the report of the Court of Enquiry . . . they have decided that you shall appear before a Court Martial to answer a charge.'

This was specified later as follows:

[4] Lumby.

'For that he ... Rear-Admiral Ernest Charles Thomas Troubridge, Royal Navy, C.B., C.M.G., M.V.O., having command of His Majesty's First Cruiser Squadron, then being a person subject to the Naval Discipline Act, did, on the 7th day of August, 1914, from negligence or through other default, forbear to pursue the chase of His Imperial Majesty's ship *Goeben*, being an enemy then flying.'

For the great-grandson of a favoured member of Nelson's 'band of brothers', these words must have struck a fearful knell. But the Act itself contained yet more alarming phrases:

'Every officer who shall forbear to pursue the chase of any enemy ... beaten or flying ... or who shall improperly forsake his station shall, if he has therein acted traitorously, suffer death; if he has acted from cowardice suffer death ... if he has acted from negligence ... shall be dismissed from His Majesty's Service, with disgrace, or shall suffer such other punishment as is hereinafter mentioned.'

From the clear recollection of the Prosecutor, Rear-Admiral Sydney Fremantle, we know that opinion in the Admiralty was running strongly against Troubridge, and that pressure was put on Fremantle to try him on a charge of cowardice, this option being open to the Prosecutor. But Troubridge's reputation for physical courage was impeccable, and indeed famous.

'I came to the conclusion that it would be quite impossible to prove cowardice, and I flatly refused to inflict on such an officer the indignity of ever being tried on such a charge.'[5]

This was the response of a man of discernment and integrity. But that he was even solicited to frame a harsher charge is itself indication of remarkable venom.

It was against this background that Troubridge set out on his *via dolorosa*.

[5] *My Naval Career.*

12

Court Martial...the Case for the Prosecution

'Bravery and Loyalty were insufficient Securities for the Life and Honour of a Naval Officer.' MEMORIAL TO ADM. BYNG

A NY Court Martial in wartime, however humble the accused or trivial the charge, imposes on a perceptive onlooker a strange and indelible impression. There is an air of total commitment to the cause of justice, due to an awareness that for non-lawyers such a trial is fraught with traps and uncertainties— with the ultimate hazard of a possible miscarriage of justice.

All the circumstances on this almost unparalleled occasion were formidable. The Court sat in the President's Flagship, HMS *Bulwark*,[1] at Portland; The President was Admiral Sir George Le Clerc Egerton, Commander-in-Chief of His Majesty's Ships and Vessels at the Hamoaze and in Plymouth Sound. With him sat four other admirals and four captains, with the Deputy Judge-Advocate as adviser on legal matters. The Warrant was signed by Sir William Graham Greene, Secretary to Their Lordships, and two of the Sea Lords, being Commissioners for executing the Office of the Lord High Admiral of the United Kingdom of Great Britain and Ireland, etc. The accused was represented by Mr Leslie Scott, KC, MP, barrister-at-law, as 'The Accused's

---

[1] Later that month *Bulwark* blew up, from an internal explosion, probably due to defective cordite.

113

Friend', supported by Sir Henry Johnson, solicitor. The Prosecutor was Rear-Admiral Sydney Fremantle.

Scott was a lawyer of great standing, who in 1922 became Solicitor-General. He belonged to the gifted generation that included Rufus Isaacs and F. E. Smith—though his distinction was hardly comparable to theirs. Between 1909 and 1926 he was the official representative of HM Government at the International Conferences on Maritime Law. In 1922 he was knighted, and five years later was made a Privy Councillor. He was finally, for many years, a Lord Justice of Appeal. It might be safe to credit him with an attractive sense of humour, since he chose young A. P. Herbert as his Private Secretary soon after the Great War.

It was clear that the full pomp and expertise both of the Law and the Senior Service were to be deployed.

The Court was closed only during certain periods 'in the interests of the State', but there were no newspaper reporters. This was due not to an official embargo, but to the surprising circumstance that none applied for permission to attend. What they missed, the actual words spoken, might never have been disclosed; for only by a special dispensation of the Ministry of Defence has the customary restriction on Military Courts Martial been lately lifted in this case.

Captain Wray was the first witness; but at this stage his task was merely to swear to the logs of *Defence* for August; he was followed by Commander Marston, a Navigation expert, for the prosecution. Very soon the evidence was centred on secret matters, and the public were ordered to withdraw. Marston's evidence dealt entirely with the relative courses of *Defence* and *Goeben*.

The man whom all were eager to see, though for different reasons, was the key witness, Sir Berkeley Milne himself. His dispositons and actions had already been officially 'cleared' by Their Lordships in strangely generous terms—and it was to be expected that he could well afford to show a similar generosity towards the accused. Almost at once, inadvertently one hopes, he referred to the recent Court of Enquiry, and received a sharp rebuke from the Deputy Judge-Advocate: 'No witness should mention that fact. It is detrimental to the accused.' Soon Leslie Scott, KC, was in difficulties with the President, being denied access to the log of Milne's flagship. A partial concession was made, and 'relevant' matter from the log was cleared for the defence to see.

Milne was asked, 'Did you give the accused any reason to suppose that the two battle cruisers would rejoin his flag?' 'None.' But he did admit that the Admiralty signal about 'a superior force' was ambiguous. Yet he believed that on 6/7 August Troubridge should have continued on his dawn course till he sighted the *Goeben*. Milne expected the Cruiser Squadron to make contact, and had received Troubridge's signal (referring to a 6 am meeting) which confirmed this belief.

Scott now took up his first vital cross-examination. Milne was swiftly under pressure:

Scott: 'The battle cruisers are necessarily, by reason of their guns and speed, more adequate for dealing with the *Goeben* than armoured cruisers—ship for ship?'

Milne: 'It depends upon numbers. Six ships must be better than four.'

S: 'I am not dealing with numbers. I am asking you as to individual ships. The battle cruiser is obviously more suited than the armoured cruiser, apart from numbers, for meeting with the *Goeben*?'

M: 'Certainly.'

S: 'And the Admiralty evidently thought it desirable not only to have one battle cruiser but two battle cruisers to deal with the *Goeben*?'

M: 'One battle cruiser might be faster than the other.'

S: 'I am asking what is the reasonable inference for you as Commander-in-Chief to draw from this Admiralty telegram. Was it not fairly plain that the Admiralty held the view that it was desirable to have two battle cruisers at hand to deal with the *Goeben*?'

M : 'It may have meant that.'

S : 'And the instructions as to the approach to the Adriatic are quite clear? There is no ambiguity in them. It is to be watched by cruisers and destroyers?'

M : 'Yes.'

Shortly after this passage, the President was asked by Scott if he could look at the secret war orders to see what might be material to the defence. The President merely said : 'They cannot be produced in any case.' Again there were questions that concerned the French fleet. The Court asked : 'Is this relevant?' Scott replied that there were special reasons, and added : 'You appreciate that?' The President : 'No. I do not.'

As the questioning turned towards the well-worn subject of comparative force, Scott asked Milne : 'What are the chief elements that enter into this question of a comparative force?' To which the absurd answer came : 'Gun power, weather, and speed. I do not know of anything else.' Even the astute Scott missed the fairly glaring omission—Milne made no reference to armour. Captain Creswell, to whom I am indebted for this particular point, remarks ironically that 'as far as Milne was concerned, Troubridge's ships could have been built of tin'.

One of the oddest features of the trial was the enormous emphasis on gunnery in contrast to the near total omission of the factor of armour.

The figures speak for themselves : against the *Goeben*'s maximum of 11 inches, *Defence* and her sister ships had a maximum of 6 inches at the water line, and their deck protection ranged from $1\frac{1}{2}$ inches to a meagre $\frac{3}{4}$ inch thickness.

In due course Milne was brought to the question of a possible night attack by Troubridge, but Milne conceded that he had ordered this to be left to the destroyers. So yet again the definition of a 'superior force' was raised.

13. HMS *Defence* in Malta Harbour, 1913

14. HMS *Agincourt* (foreground) and HMS *Erin* (previously *Sultan Osman I* and *Rashadieh*)

15. *Yavuz* spick and span after a major refit

16. *Yavuz* at Gölcük, Sea of Marmora, from a cine-film taken in July, 1972

Scott: 'The Admiralty gave you instructions to avoid being engaged with superior force?'

Milne: 'Yes.'

S: 'Did they leave you to judge whether any force was superior or not?'

M: 'Well, I suppose so.'

S: 'Anyhow, the man on the spot was the best judge: if you were on the spot—you; and if the Rear-Admiral was on the spot—then he?'

M: 'Yes.'

But as the strenuous questioning proceeded Milne fell back more and more on evasive answers.

Scott put it to him that the ship with a 5-knot advantage in speed was the absolute master as regards range, and elaborated the theme; Milne was forced to agree.

Milne claimed to be unaware that the *Goeben*'s guns, at full elevation of $30°$, could shoot 25,000 to 30,000 yards, and answered 'I am not aware of it.' 'Would you regard Sir Percy Scott as an expert?' 'Yes. He is a gunnery man.' (This was not unlike reluctantly admitting that Einstein *was* a mathematician —since Admiral Scott was famous in his day as the ultimate authority on this subject.) Admiral Scott had written a letter which clearly stated that with an elevation of $30°$ and a muzzle velocity of 3,090 feet per second *Goeben*'s guns would have a range of nearly 30,000 yards (15 sea miles). But Admiral Scott was not available, and the President declined to allow his letter to be given in evidence.

Milne continued to be non-commital about the relative range of the opposing guns, till Scott cornered him with:

'I press for an answer. Have you formed the opinion and hold it to-day that there is not a serious or big difference between the effective range of the two forces?'

Milne's feeble response was, 'There is not a big difference.' And so Milne, with this false premise behind him, continued to claim that Troubridge should have gone on—should have 'done it properly'.

Then Milne was asked to work out in Court on the chart on what course the cruisers should have steamed to make contact. But the President intervened: 'I don't think it is quite fair . . . that the witness should be called upon to work this out.'

S : 'The Admiral [Milne] has expressed the opinion that the Rear-Admiral ought to have continued and engaged the *Goeben* . . . It is a very, very serious charge.'

The President: 'He has given his opinion. Are you not satisfied with that?'

S : 'Very much not. I hope to convince the Court it is the wrong opinion.'

This was indeed the crux, and Milne was about to be 'saved by the bell'.

P : 'You are trying to prove this opinion by a paper thing done on the chart.'

S : 'I am trying to test it. If he wants time, I shall be anxious to make any concession.'

P : 'His opinion has been given.'

S : 'I want now to test it to show it is baseless.'

P : 'Better ask the question then, not ask him to work out a problem.'

S : 'I have asked the question.'

P : 'And he has answered it.'

S : 'I am in the hands of the Court. You appreciate . . .'

But at this point Admiral Egerton had had enough, and Scott was cut short a little brusquely. However, he was not the man to let a floundering witness off the hook.

P : 'You, I understand, blame the Rear-Admiral—is that right?'

S : 'Yes.'

P : 'You blame him, not because he failed to sight the *Goeben* that night, but because he let the *Goeben* escape. Is that right or not?'

S : 'In a way, yes; and in a way, no.'

The next part of the cross-examination dealt with the effect of having no battle cruisers with him and how this influenced his actions. Milne agreed that these big ships would have made success certain. Finally, as the first day drew to a close, Scott pressed Milne to admit that he himself could have caught the German ships at Messina with a proper disposition of his three capital ships. This cogent and awkward question elicited no reply.

On the second day Milne was back in the witness box, and Scott took him in detail through the signal Troubridge had sent at noon on the 7th to explain his abandoning the chase. On hearing his version of all this, the Court grew uneasy, to the extent that the Deputy Judge-Advocate warned Milne that he was not bound to answer any question which might incriminate himself. This strikes one as curious, since the Admiralty had long issued a blanket statement expressing their approbation of Milne's performance—so he was surely immune to any disciplinary action.

What is so painfully evident as one reads the whole cross-examination is the complete indifference shown by Milne towards his loyal subordinate. The contrast is sharp and revealing. Troubridge was prepared to go to great lengths to avoid all derogatory comments on Milne, while his Commander-in-Chief was busy protecting his own skin, and even adding to Troubridge's difficulties. Fisher's rude sobriquet, 'Sir B. Mean', begins to take on a new significance.

But again the earlier critical question was posed :

S : 'Would you not have forced [*Goeben*] to action much more easily if you had had a battle cruiser at each end of the Straits [of Messina]?'

M : 'No, I do not think so, for this reason. Owing to speed, the *Goeben* would have come out at a very high speed, probably pass the battle cruiser and be away before she could get up her full speed.'

Scott repeated the question still more precisely and received an equally unconvincing reply.

As the last question before they adjourned for lunch—and one can't help wondering who lunched with whom—Scott asked:

S : 'If you wanted him to engage without battle cruisers, knowing the orders he had that he was not to get seriously engaged with a superior force, why didn't you tell him plainly, under the existing circumstances, you must take all risks and engage her?'

M : 'I thought it perfectly unnecessary.'

After lunch Milne was questioned by members of the Court:

'Did you give any orders to the Rear-Admiral to attack the *Goeben* if he met her?'

M : 'No, because we were at war, and I did not consider it necessary to give any orders to His Majesty's officers to attack the enemy.'

The rest of the afternoon and much of the next day was occupied with Fawcet Wray's evidence, most of which has already been covered. One of his answers crystallized his gunnery credo.

'Up to the range of 16,000 yards the *Goeben* must be a superior force to one *Defence* or four *Defences* ... For four ships to try to attack her is first of all impossible because you could not get to the 16,000 yards [*sic*] unless she wanted you to, but if you did get within 16,000, or 20,000 yards if you like, it is suicidal.'

One answer determined beyond ambiguity what Wray felt about his Admiral's reaction to the crisis:

Scott : 'I want his demeanour in the early part of the morning, when the orders of the Fleet to this squadron were with a view to an action at 6 in the morning?'

Wray : 'His one object in life was to fight.'

S : 'And when he changed his mind he was extraordinarily distressed by having to come to that decision?'

W : 'Extraordinarily so.'

The last witness for the prosecution was a gunnery expert, Commander Franklin, employed in the Ordnance Department at the Admiralty. His evidence, naturally, was of the most technical character, and reads like an extract from an advanced text-book. However, one answer is illuminating :

Scott : 'Will you give the total weight of one round of broadside from the *Goeben* and one from the First Cruiser Squadron, respectively.

Franklin : '*Goeben*, 6,720 lb. First Cruiser Squadron, 7,480 lb.'

Scott's final question elicited a most helpful reply.

S : 'You, in command of the *Goeben*, would be superior to them?' [the four British cruisers]

F : 'Yes.'

S : 'You have no doubt that the *Goeben* could do that at 17,000 yards?'

F : 'I have no doubt.'

Fremantle, in re-examination of his witness, covered the question of accuracy at long range, and recorded that one battleship, the *Conqueror*, the earliest of the Dreadnoughts to be equipped with 13.5-inch guns, during a practice shoot at 18,000 yards scored not a single hit out of forty rounds. To this the President gloomily asserted : 'In that case the German guns must be better than ours.'

Very shortly after this important concession, the prosecution was closed. The accused was informed by the Judge-Advocate that he might give evidence, but warned 'that he would thereby render himself liable to cross-examination'. Troubridge then applied to give evidence. But it was 5 pm on the Saturday, and the Court was adjourned until Monday morning, 9 November.

13

Troubridge's Defence

'The odious task of explaining.' ADMIRAL TROUBRIDGE

UNLIKE the usual procedure in a civil trial, the defence opened, not with an introduction by Counsel, but with a lengthy survey of his whole case by the Accused. Troubridge's statement, which he read himself, so lucidly sets out his case, and so clearly reflects the man, his background, his moral standards and his cruel dilemma, that it deserves to be quoted very fully. There may be passages that owe much to Scott's skilful drafting, but the words reveal better than any mere précis the true character of the accused.

'Before opening my defence to the charge that has been preferred against me, I beg I may be permitted to state to the Court that for the first six weeks of this great war I was in command of a force of His Majesty's ships employed on a close watch or blockade of an enemy's coast, one of the most arduous and responsible services that can fall to an Admiral in these days. For a great part of this time I have carried out this service against what is worse than a declared enemy—an undeclared enemy [the Austrians], whose transition from the latter to the former would in all probability take the form of a sudden and treacherous attack upon my forces.

'The incidents which form the subject of this charge occurred on 6 and 7 August.

'Before entering into the details of my own actions and

decisions I beg to lay before the Court two general propositions for their consideration :

'1. When an officer in command of a fleet, or a squadron, or a military force, is ordered by a superior authority to avoid being brought to action by an enemy it is clear that in his obedience he may risk thereby his reputation for all that an officer holds dear. The superior authority who has issued such an order is, therefore, bound in all honour to support in his action the officer who acts in obedience to such an order—the most difficult and unwelcome that it is possible for an officer to receive. Every officer knows well that the vast majority of his fellow-countrymen are not in a position to consider or appreciate the intricacies of naval warfare or questions of superiority or inferiority of force, or the reasons for it. Secret orders cannot be published broadcast : only a very general idea of such matters as battles or engagements comes within the purview of the general public. The ulterior objects with which such secret orders are given, the great, and often distant, objectives of a war on a grand scale, and the subordination to such objectives of all minor issues, all these are left to the high authorities.

'On the other hand, the applause and appreciation of one's fellow-countrymen, whatever may be the value of the criticism, is dear to us who risk our all to serve them, and may even, and often does, compensate for official censure, so long as the officers concerned have actually engaged or been brought to action by the enemy.'

It is relevant to remember that the dreadful news of Coronel, where Rear-Admiral Sir Christopher Cradock's light squadron, heroically facing a clearly preponderant force, had been annihilated by von Spee, had reached England only a week earlier. Gallantry, when it led to utter defeat in the first important action by the Royal Navy for many decades, was quickly recognized as a very mixed virtue.

Troubridge continued in one of the most moving paragraphs ever penned by a British admiral:

'Of all the orders to an officer, those directing him or permitting him to attack an enemy under all circumstances and at all costs, are the most agreeable. *Such orders are easy and simple, and, whatever the issue, he must receive the applause of those who know little and the approval of those who know much.* (Author's italics). The more superior the enemy force the greater the honour of victory, the greater the honour of death. But the order to *avoid* being brought to action by an enemy is of all orders the most trying for an officer to receive.

'2. Where an officer commanding a fleet, or a squadron, or a military force, or any units thereof, receives from superior authority orders directing him to avoid being brought to action *by a superior force of the enemy*, then in the absence of any precise instructions for his guidance, it is clear that he may at any moment be called upon to decide what, in his judgement, constituted a superior force. An officer, therefore, in receipt of such orders clearly understands that, in obedience to them, he binds himself to risk his honour and his reputation in their fulfilment. So grave is the possible result to him, that the superior authority asking of him so great a possible sacrifice must be equally bound to accept, and to support the honest, reasonable and considered judgement on this point of the officer to whom the orders have been given—*even* (and I desire to emphasise this point) in the event of his judgement not meeting with the full concurrence of the superior authority, and *even* if the after consequences of his decision, unforeseen at the moment, prove vexatious to the superior authority, or adversely affect the general policy of the country.

'This is the double bond that binds the authority giving such orders to the officer who receives them. The grave risk, the great responsibility accepted by the officer receiving such orders, has its counterpart in the risk and responsibility by the superior authority upon his honest, reasonable and considered judgement. Without such mutual reliance no such orders can ever be given in war; or, if given, can never be expected to be obeyed.'

This impressive assertion of the principle of reciprocal loyalty would be hard to dispute. It was also a discreet pointer towards that shared responsibility which the Admiralty had shown little desire to shoulder. Twenty-six years later the same First Lord, at a moment of crisis, gave a daring destroyer flotilla commander a directive, carrying a clear acceptance of this vital principle. Captain Warburton-Lee off the Norwegian coast in April 1940 was told :

'Proceed to Narvik and sink or capture enemy ship. [There were ten.] It is at your discretion to land forces, if you think you can recapture Narvik from number of enemy present.'

A little later a further message was sent—the last. It read :

'Norwegian coast defence vessels may be in German hands : *you alone can judge* whether in these circumstances attack should be made. *Shall support whatever decision you take.*' (Author's italics.)

In the event Warburton-Lee launched an attack that cost him his ship and his life and earned him the Victoria Cross.

Churchill's intervention, short-circuiting the chain of command, has been stigmatized as 'an extraordinary act'—which, despite Churchill's belief that he was giving the flotilla commander a free choice, made an heroic but wasteful response virtually certain.[1]

Be that as it may, it is clear that Churchill had travelled a long way since 1914, that according to his lights he was far more flexible in his instructions, and that he had abandoned the fatal habit of drafting crucial signals in his own hand. Perhaps certain memories of 1914 were present in his mind as he and his First Sea Lord promised support—'whatever decision you take'.

[1] Letter from Captain Stephen Roskill to the author, 10 January, 1973.

Troubridge now ventured two examples to illustrate his two opening propositions. The first referred to a controversial retirement by the highly aggressive Japanese commander during the Russo-Japanese war of 1904 (at which, as we know, Troubridge had been an official observer). Admiral Togo had withdrawn his fleet after a preliminary bombardment of Port Arthur.

'To such a pitch did this [withdrawal] excite the feelings within Admiral Togo's command that the comments in the fleet on his conduct were very severe. Plots to assassinate him were talked of . . . But one thing, *and one thing only*, sustained him.'

The supreme command publicly approved his seemingly over-cautious conduct and upheld his honour and reputation.

'The second example I would give is nearer home. A squadron of our cruisers has recently been lost in battle . . . The *Aboukir* was sunk by a submarine [on 22 September]. Her consorts, the *Hogue* and the *Cressy*, regardless of the danger from what was clearly under the circumstances a superior force of the enemy, at once closed the sinking ship and putting out their boats, proceeded to rescue their drowning comrades, with a gallantry and fidelity that has found an echo throughout the country. The Admiralty, in a communication to the Fleet, has stated that in their opinion, an error of judgement was committed, in that these ships were thus exposed to attack from what proved to be a superior force . . . The Admiralty added that in future such a procedure should not be carried and that ships in company should not expose themselves for such a purpose to such a disaster.

'What is here intended is perfectly clear; it means that the error in judgement on the part of the officers concerned lay in the fact that they did not make the great decision to avoid battle with the enemy, even though they must thereby let their comrades in the *Aboukir* perish, and thereby place their reputations in jeopardy. Further, the Admiralty demand in future the same great decision from any of us naval officers.

'There is only one condition under which such great decisions *can* be demanded of us, and that is *the* absolute certainty that whichever course an officer's honest judgement dictates, whether it subsequently prove right or prove wrong, the Admiralty, who ask of him to take so great a risk to his reputation, must in their turn take upon them the responsibility of his resulting action. And no doubt they will.'

As a matter of interest, the Court of Enquiry on the loss of the three ancient *Cressys* blamed a War Staff telegram for their ill-planned patrol, and it has since been established that this was sent by Sturdee as COS, without Churchill's knowledge.

Troubridge now moved on to relate his two propositions to the events under investigation.

'I desire to refer to my own position in the approaches to the Adriatic after I left Malta on the evening of 2 August. My orders were to shadow the *Goeben* and *Breslau* with the two battle cruisers and to watch the entrance of the Adriatic with the cruisers, reporting at once if the Austrian fleet came out. The force placed under my command to fulfil this service was:

> Two battle cruisers for the first object
> Two light cruisers ⎫
> Some destroyers ⎬ for the second object
> Four cruisers   ⎭

'The orders . . . were that it was important to husband these forces in the early stages of the war, and to avoid being brought to action by a superior force of the enemy. The almost immediate hostility of Austria and Germany was assumed: the attitude of Italy was described as doubtful, and I was ordered not to approach the Italian coast, being further verbally warned by the Commander-in-Chief to take care of the Italian fleet at Taranto.

'On 3 August the battle cruisers were despatched to shadow

the *Goeben*, as I will describe later. I was, of course, not aware of what everyone now knows—that war with Austria would be delayed for a week, and that Italy would decide to remain neutral. On the contrary I was bound to assume and to allow for all the worst contingencies. It was, therefore, perfectly clear to me from the beginning that this question of what constituted a superior force might at any moment arise. If the Austrian or the Italian fleet, or both, intended to come out, as was expected, and to threaten the French operation of transporting their African army to Marseilles, they would certainly begin by attempting to drive me from my station of operations. The German force consisted of one battle cruiser and one light cruiser. The Italians had a division of the fleet at Taranto. The main strength of the Austrian fleet consisted, generally, of twelve battleships and two armoured cruisers ... I had, therefore, to be prepared to sight ... a large number of different combinations of the enemy ships, of which combinations some might properly be considered as inferior, some equal, some superior. And it is not only in actual material that the quality or otherwise might be a question for my decision. Their destroyers might be in harbours not far distant or mine might be near at hand. I might meet them in the morning or the evening, in thick weather or fine weather—in short, every circumstance of the sea, which will readily occur to members of the Court, might be matter, at the moment of sighting the enemy, to influence me in the great decision I would be called upon to make.

'All this I clearly saw and understood; and I accepted the responsibility, both because it was my duty and because I felt absolutely certain that my reputation would be safe in the hands of my superior authorities, who I did not doubt would protect me from any injurious imputations that might follow in the event of my deciding on that course which is, and always must be, repugnant to a British officer, viz. to avoid being brought to action.'

However, Troubridge saw the case of a battle cruiser in opposition to a cruiser squadron as a special one.

'On this subject I held, and do hold, clear and definite opinions. It was my duty as Rear-Admiral to assess the value in war of all possible antagonists to my squadron; and having commanded a squadron of cruisers for eighteen months, I had long made up my mind that the question whether a modern battle cruiser, as compared with a cruiser squadron, was to be considered a superior force must depend on circumstances. She is not superior if the squadron can get within their range of her to open an engagement.'

This was indeed what Troubridge held to be, factually and realistically, the crux of his case.

'But their ability to do so depends upon various circumstances : the distance at which the visibility of the atmosphere will allow her to be sighted, the time of day or of night, the navigational conditions owing to proximity of land or shoal waters. Under such circumstances (if favourable) the squadron will have a chance of neutralizing her initial elements of superiority, consisting in superior speed, and greater gun range. Conversely, a modern battle cruiser is a superior force to a cruiser squadron, if on a day of perfect visibility she is sighted in the open sea, where she can utilize to the full the benefit of all the tactical elements designed to make her a superior force to cruisers, while they cannot reach her with their guns. I trust that this comparison between a battle cruiser and a cruiser squadron will not cause it to be thought for a moment that (orders apart) I would not, with great pleasure, have permitted a battle cruiser to engage me. On the contrary, I well know the fortunes and chances of war, and the greater satisfaction that ensues from an engagement with a superior force.'

This brought him to the emotional heart of the matter, and surely no one in court can have doubted the absolute sincerity of his words.

'I and the gallant officers of my squadron would have asked no more than to be allowed to do what we could and take our chance of the result; indeed, with only two ships; or even with the *Defence* alone. We had often discussed it. But such desires and ambitions could not alter the main fact that in my measured opinion as a responsible Flag Officer, a cruiser squadron allowing itself to be sighted by a battle cruiser under such conditions as have been described, would allow itself to be brought to battle by a superior force of the enemy.

'My opinions as to the relative value of these types of ships were known to my Commander-in-Chief, and, at his request, I lectured on them to the Officers of the Fleet on board of his flagship last October [1913].'

Troubridge then recapitulated his movements, orders and discussions with his Commander-in-Chief—most of which will now be familiar. He continued:

'It is painful to me to break through the habits of a life-time and criticize the actions of my superior officer. But the gravity of the charge against me leaves me with no alternative. I must allude to the Commander-in-Chief's disposition of the fleet and the effect it had later in influencing my mental attitude and my decisions.

'My sailing orders are before the Court. I was to take under my command a certain force, namely, two battle cruisers, my cruiser squadron, and some light vessels, and I was to carry out the orders contained in an Admiralty telegram attached, the duties of each unit being clearly defined. *The two battle cruisers were to shadow the Goeben. The armoured cruisers were to watch the Adriatic* and report if the Austrian fleet came out. Now if I may comment on the orders of the Admiralty, I permit myself to say that I considered these orders admirably designed to fulfil the objects in view. They were brief, simple, and easily understood, and I say, without fear of contradiction, that had they never been departed from, the *Goeben* would inevitably have been brought to battle . . .

'Now the Court will recollect that the Admiralty orders which the Commander-in-Chief had directed me to carry out, were to shadow the *Goeben* with the two battle-cruisers. When they had got in touch, the Admiralty had ordered her to be *held*. Though the fulfilment of these orders could not be guaranteed when the *Goeben* was at large and her position unknown, now that she was located at Messina, they appeared to be easy of fulfilment. She was only a few hours distant from the battle cruisers, and I took it for granted they would at once proceed to shadow her and to hold her. It was with feelings of dismay that I found this was not done. My command had been tacitly, and of course legitimately, taken from me by the Commander-in-Chief, who was now directing the whole operation. I knew little of what was going on except from intercepted messages some of which were only replies. One thing seemed clear. The battle cruisers were to the west. I could not with propriety make any suggestion to the Commander-in-Chief. But he knew my secret orders and my opinion also on the subject of superior force.

'At 1.30 pm[2] on 5 August I had made the following to him: "In case *Goeben* is in these waters I am keeping within 30 miles of Santa Maura [or Levkas, a little south of Corfu]. If we encounter her I shall endeavour to draw her into narrow waters where we can engage her at our range."

'I was convinced that the west was barred by the French, in which surmise I was correct.'

Troubridge then explained how he had met the French Admiral Lapeyrère eleven days later, and found him retrospectively in precise agreement with his own tactical thinking. Again he stressed that he could see no reason why Milne should not have used his battle cruisers to hold the *Goeben* in the Straits of Messina.

'I determined to endeavour to bring the *Goeben* to action that night [5 August] if she left Messina. The weather was calm

2 All times have been converted to Central European Time.

and very clear and down the full moon nearly as bright as day. I steamed over to the Italian coast, took up a position there with the squadron, and gave the necessary orders. By keeping on the dark side I hoped to close her to a useful range. She did not, however, leave Messina, and I resumed my usual station. The Commander-in-Chief signalled to me at 7.19 pm to use the destroyers for night work, by which I understood I was *not* to use the cruisers; so I did not repeat the operation.

'On 6 August I expected all day to hear of the Commander-in-Chief coming east, and effecting a junction with me before Messina. The *Goeben* had a speed of $3\frac{1}{2}$ knots above the battle cruisers, so that what was wanted to bring her to action was a broad front in narrow waters. But as the day passed without his doing so, I took up a position to intercept the *Goeben* before daybreak, or, alternatively, to be ready to meet the Commander-in-Chief should he come east.

'At about 6 pm the *Goeben* was reported by the *Gloucester* as having left Messina and to be steering east. After rounding Spartivento she shaped a course for the entrance to the Adriatic. The *Gloucester*, brilliantly shadowing, reported her course and speed continually.'

Troubridge then came to the evidence, that has already been mentioned, of aiming to fight the *Goeben* in shoal waters off Fano Island, just west of Corfu; this would assist in choosing his own range. When news came through to him from the *Gloucester* that *Goeben* was shaping south-east, Troubridge believed that this was a feint, since he could at that time see no sense (from Souchon's point of view) in continuing towards eastern waters.

'The Court will realize that there is nothing so difficult as surmising the destination of a fleet or a ship that had broken a blockade. Nelson's letters and despatches show in pages and pages how, when Bruix got away from Brest, Nelson closely reasoned and argued the matter, and how difficult it was for him to decide upon their probable destination. Three times by signal and also in my written orders I had been ordered to prevent her getting to the Adriatic. She had already been to the west to Bona [Bône], and for some reason had returned east to Messina.'

He explained, as we already have seen, how, soon after mid-night on 6 August he turned south,

'hoping that something might occur, some change of course and speed that would enable me to intercept her before day-light. I also knew that the *Dublin* (which with two destroyers was joining my flag from Malta) hoped to fall in with her about 2.30 am. I thought the *Dublin*'s attack might turn her towards me . . .

'By now I had realized that if the *Goeben*'s objective was in the direction of her present course [i.e. not a feint] I had kept too far north, and lost the chance of closing her in the dark so as to engage her at dawn. Nevertheless I still continued on my southerly course with the intention of engaging her, even though it looked as if I could probably only do it under the very conditions which I knew made it my duty not to do it; and I signalled accordingly. It was this: I could not say so, *but my deep conviction was that the Goeben had no right to be escaping at all* [author's italics], and that if she had been sealed up in the Straits of Messina by the battle cruisers, as I thought she ought to have been, she never would have escaped. As I said to my Flag Captain: "The Mediterranean will stink if we don't attack her."

'It was a desperate decision and contrary to my orders, but I made it (as stated by Captain Wray in his evidence), and for a time I stuck to it. Gradually, however, it forced itself more and more upon my mind that though my decision might be natural, might be heroic, it was certainly wrong and cer-tainly in the teeth of my orders. The result was, that after a mental struggle between my natural desire to fight and my sense of duty in view of my orders, I came to the conclusion that I was not justified in allowing her to bring me to battle under the conditions in which we should sight one another.

It was at this psychological moment, or rather just as I was reaching this conclusion, that my Flag Captain came back to me and the conversation he has given in evidence took place. It was a most difficult and delicate duty for my subordinate officer to take, but it was his duty; and, as a matter of fact, I did in reality completely agree with the representations he made to me. After he left me I thought it over a little further and then I made my decision.'

So at 3.55 am he signalled to the *Dublin* and *Gloucester* that he must abandon the chase. We do not know the immediate reaction of the ardent Kelly brothers, with their Irish passion for a fight; but it was probably savage.

Troubridge's statement now turned at some length to review the tactical issues arising from a superior force with greater speed and greater range of guns.

'For a year I had been thinking how, by skill in tactics or by guile and subtlety, I could get over the fact that, on a day of perfect visibility in the open sea, a battle cruiser could open and continue a fire upon us from a distance of 8 miles and upwards, while the squadron remained a passive target held, whether chasing or retiring, at a constant range . . .

'I believe my Flag Captain's evidence, that the *Goeben* can shoot effectively at 20,000 to 24,000 yards, is correct . . .

'For this reason I designed to meet her at night, or at dawn, or in narrow waters, or, in fact, under any conditions under which I could engage her within my own range and counter-act the tactical advantages of speed and range.'

Troubridge then had something cogent to say about Milne's evidence.

'The Commander-in-Chief, having assumed that there was no disparity between the range of the *Goeben*'s guns and ours, was logical in his opinion that, although she could not be forced into action against her will, I might nevertheless have gone on and, at any rate, sighted her that morning. If there had been no such disparity this might have been a proper course to adopt, because on his assumption, if I had been brought to battle it would not have been against an obviously superior force. But a great disparity having (as I submit) been conclusively proved, the Commander-in-Chief's argument entirely falls to the ground.'

According to his orders Troubridge had no right to put himself in a position where he no longer had it in his power to *avoid* being brought to action.

'If the Commander-in-Chief is wrong in thinking that there was no difference between the range of the *Goeben*'s guns and ours, it necessarily follows that he was wrong in saying that "I ought to have gone on that morning and at any rate sighted her".'

As the accused drew towards the conclusion of the whole matter he was able to remind the Court that both the expert gunnery witnesses, one for the prosecution and his own Flag Captain, had affirmed that the *Goeben* greatly outranged the smaller cruisers, probably by 5,000 yards, an even greater difference than Troubridge had stated in *Defence*'s log. Now he came to his tense and moving peroration :

'Since my return to England I have heard many stories about this affair, many extravagant, many outrageous, none true.

'None of my superiors could divulge the secret orders under which I acted. Nor, Sir, could I. They have remained secret as far as I have been concerned, and I have silently endured the consequences even to this day when I am here with the odious task of explaining to my brother officers on this Court why I did not go to battle.

'In our service we all risk our lives for our country every day and give no thought to it. Our ancestors have done it for generations—our sons are doing it to-day.

'But here, in the first days of this great war much more is asked of me. In obedience to orders to avoid being brought to battle I am asked to risk my honour and the honour of the great name I bear. There was a moment—I have said it—when I felt too much was asked of me; I could not do it. Then I reflected. I felt that was unworthy of me. If my country asked it of me then even my honour I would imperil. And so, Sir, I leave it in your hands.'

14

Cross-examination and Finding

'The Commander-in-Chief did not like suggestions.'
TROUBRIDGE

TROUBRIDGE's statement, which he had begun at 9.45 on Monday morning, ended seventy minutes later. Scott rose to say, 'The accused tenders himself for cross-examination.' The Court was then cleared while it considered the statement. There was a slightly absurd wrangle as to whether all Troubridge's comments could be regarded as 'sworn'; the Deputy Judge-Advocate said, 'I take it the prosecutor or the Court can ask the accused if the whole statement is true.' To this Troubridge responded: 'I know he [the prosecutor] can ask me any question in the world and I am prepared to swear to anything in the defence.'

This ended the preliminary skirmishes. Then came a number of questions mainly related to Milne's failure to guard the Straits of Messina. What followed was bound to cover ground that is already familiar; but a number of the questions and answers are of special significance.

Prosecutor: 'You received the orders "*Goeben* is your objective, and the primary consideration". If *Goeben* was a superior force how do you reconcile those orders with the governing order not to get engaged with a superior force?'

Troubridge: 'Because at that time I had the whole Mediterranean Fleet except *Inflexible* under my command.'

P: 'Then did the orders become irreconcilable after the two battle cruisers had left you?'

T: 'The *Goeben* was their objective, but they left me to shadow her and then to hold her.'

P: 'Do I understand that you considered the orders that the *Goeben* was your primary consideration did no longer apply to you after the battle cruisers had left you?'

T: 'Certainly I do not. I should like you to tell me what "objective" means.'

P: 'I suggest that the the order that the *Goeben* was your objective and primary consideration was irreconcilable with the hypothesis that the *Goeben* was a superior force to the First Cruiser Squadron?'

T: 'If you suggest it that may be your opinion, but I am not prepared personally to accept it myself.'

P: 'The Commander-in-Chief assigned to you as your objective the *Goeben*. He directed you not to get seriously engaged with a superior force. Is it likely that the Commander-in-Chief would have given you those two orders if he had considered the *Goeben* a superior force to you, under any conditions?'

T: 'Yes, I think it quite likely.'

P: 'Did you consider that the Commander-in-Chief's signal to use destroyers for night work implied that he supposed you yourself would endeavour to engage the *Goeben* by day?'

T: 'No, I took it to mean he did not wish me to be in the middle of the night engaging the *Goeben*.'

Then came an attempt to read Milne's intentions during the critical night of 6/7 August.

P: 'Were not your signals in conjunction with those of the *Gloucester* such as to lead the Commander-in-Chief to believe you were proceeding to engage the *Goeben*?'

This was a little awkward to answer, since with a proper rapport between the two senior officers the likely reply should be 'yes'. Troubridge could not risk antagonizing the Court with a sharp answer, so merely said :

T : 'I do not really think I can answer for what the Commander-in-Chief must have thought. Every officer has different opinions on all these things and different brains to judge from, and so on; but what *his* judgement could be I do not really think I can answer for.'

Fremantle then focused his questions on the exact timing of Troubridge's signal that he was abandoning the chase, and Milne's silence for about five hours. Troubridge made the point that all he needed was the three words : 'Continue the chase', and that this might (and indeed should have) come in a very few minutes. 'It would have been one code word. The greatest load would have been taken off my mind if he had [signalled].' And then he added that such a signal from Milne, up to 7 am, would still have allowed him to intercept the *Goeben*.

A little later in a discussion of gunnery skill Troubridge characteristically said : 'The Germans are an extremely clever and very practical people.'

And on the subject of the moral effect of a possible German victory at sea early in the war :

P : 'Since the moral effect of your possible action is brought into the case, did you consider the moral effect on your own officers and ships' companies of abandoning the chase, having once started it ?'

T : 'Yes, Sir. For those who knew it, the greatest sacrifice it is possible to make to obey orders is the best moral example.'

(Perhaps the slightly odd syntax is an indication of Troubridge's intensity of feeling.)

The questioning was now taken up by members of the Court, and centred on coaling problems. It emerged that the fuel shortages in the eight destroyers were severe. As Captain 'D' signalled, having listed the coal remaining, 'On this I cannot do much.'

Lieutenant-Commander A. B. Cunningham later recalled that only his own destroyer, *Scorpion*, and two others were left in company.

But naturally the Court wished above all to probe Troubridge's final decision.

P : 'Between midnight and 3 am on the 6th and 7th, were you in wireless touch with the Commander-in-Chief?'

T : 'Yes.'

P : 'Could you not have asked him then or at any other time whether he wished you to attack the *Goeben* with the First Cruiser Squadron in broad daylight, and in the open sea?'

T : 'Physically, yes; but morally, Sir, I think no. At that time I had so vividly in my mind the fact that he knew I considered her a superior force, that I did not think it proper to make such a signal as that to the Commander-in-Chief. I confess I had it sometimes in my mind to make lots of signals to him, but you will all understand there are things you cannot very well do. You might with one individual, and not with another. I had been a long time under the Commander-in-Chief's command, and I knew he did not like suggestions, and that sort of thing. I did not think I could do so with propriety. That is the right answer.'

This was as near as Troubridge, with his hard-tried loyalty, came to pricking the bubble of Milne's vanity.

P : 'Did you consider the *Goeben* a superior force?'

T : 'Yes, Sir, under the circumstances that I have indicated at various times, but not at all times.'

P : 'Under these circumstances will you explain the signal you made to your squadron at 2.10 am on the 7th: "I am endeavouring to cross the bows of the *Goeben* by 6 am, and intend to engage her if possible"?'

T : 'I gave an explanation of that in my defence. The fact was I felt it was too much for me. I knew I ought not to engage a superior force, and I was clear that whatever the ulterior objectives of the Admiralty were, they would mean disaster to us.'

P : 'I do not think that is the point. I am asking, seeing that you were under orders not to engage a superior force, and that you considered the *Goeben* was a superior force, under what conditions did you make the signal to your squadron that you were going to engage a superior force at 6 o'clock in the morning?'

T : 'I was endeavouring to explain I just meant to do it whether it was ordered or not; that is the long and short of it.'

P : 'Under what circumstances did you alter your determination?'

T : 'Because I went down and got out my orders and studied them. I had for a year been thinking how to get that ship in daylight. I knew I could not get near her, and I knew I had told my Commander-in-Chief I considered her in broad daylight to be a superior force, but I knew that I would be faithless to my trust, and I knew what it is difficult to realize now. I have been in the Admiralty and I have conducted the negotiations with the French, and nobody knew better than I the enormous importance they attached to the Austrian fleet coming out . . . I realized it was unworthy of me from my own personal gratification and ambitions, or whatever you may call it, to disobey these orders and risk the whole thing, to lose perhaps—whether we would or not I do not know—and to have let the *Goeben* divide the Mediterranean fleet into two halves, one strong and one weak, and let him fall on the weaker, and my Commander-in-Chief with a few battle cruisers only a few hours off. I realized I was doing it for myself only; that was the truth, the desire to do something, that was what governed me, instead of my orders and the interests of the country as a whole.'

Then came some questions leading up to whether the *Goeben* knew the British Cruiser Squadron's position. The answer was that Austrian merchant ships were sure to have given away the *Defence*'s position.

P : 'Did you consider that the *Goeben* was flying, if so who from?' (It will be recalled that the formal charge against Troubridge was his failure to chase an enemy 'flying'.)

T : 'You mean in the light of after events—or at the time?'

P : 'At the time, certainly?'

T : 'Well, I consider she was evidently going somewhere for some objective. I cannot say everything, I thought she was going to join the Austrian fleet, I should not say flying unless she was going with her best speed.'

P : 'Do you consider that it was impossible to chase, keep in touch with, or in any way interfere with the *Goeben*'s movements without being brought to action?'

T : 'No, Sir, not where she was, I mean to say except I had allowed her the opportunity of bringing me to action, I could do nothing. I understand that is what you mean. Of course, the word chase is rather difficult. I could have followed out of sight of the *Goeben*. Gradually pursuing her without her knowing it; perhaps it might subsequently have interfered with her actions, of course, but I think the general answer is "yes". Sighting her meant to me I had not avoided being brought to action.'

And at long last, after this relentless pursuit of truth, came the final question:

P : 'What was your particular object in anchoring to the south of Zante when you gave up the chase?'

T : 'To coal destroyers.'

The Accused's Friend stated that he did not wish to call any of the witnesses who had been summoned at his request for the defence. (The Accused having nothing further to offer in his Defence, the Court was cleared at 3.25 pm to consider the Finding.)

Four hours later the Court was re-opened, the Accused brought in, and the prosecutor and witnesses admitted; the public was not admitted. But all present could see how Admiral Troubridge's sword lay on the table. So the Finding was read:

'The Court finds as follows:

1. That on 2 August, 1914, the accused left Malta in accord-with the orders of the Commander-in-Chief, with the follow-ing ships in company: *Defence* (Flag), *Indomitable, Indefatigable, Duke of Edinburgh, Gloucester*, and the first and second Divisions of Destroyers, and was informed that "should we become engaged in war, it will be important at first to husband the naval force in the Mediterranean and, in the earlier stages, to avoid being brought to action against superior forces". He was also informed that *"Goeben* must be shadowed by two battle cruisers, approach to Adriatic must be watched by cruisers and destroyers. It is believed that Italy will remain neutral, but you cannot yet count absolutely on this."

2. That in compliance with these orders the accused proceeded towards the approaches to the Adriatic.

3. That at 3.19 pm on 3 August the *Indomitable* and *Indefatigable* were detached by the Commander-in-Chief and proceeded to search for the *Goeben* west of Sicily.

4. That on 4 August the *Black Prince* rejoined the First Cruiser Squadron.

5. That at 1.45 am on 5 August, the accused received the Admiralty General Signal to commence hostilities against Germany.

6. That on 5 August, at 0.31 pm, the accused received news that the Austrian fleet was cruising outside Pola, and at 4 pm that the *Goeben* was at Messina.

7. That at 6.15 pm on 6 August the accused received news that the *Goeben* had left Messina, steering east, shadowed by *Gloucester.* That after then *Goeben* and possibly *Breslau* were steering north 50° east towards the Adriatic. The accused's action in proposing to arrive at Fano Island at daylight next day was justifiable.

8. That at 11 pm on 6 August the accused was informed by *Gloucester* that *Goeben* was going to the south-east. That at

that time his position was north 86 east, 145 miles from the *Goeben*, approximately.

That at that time the battle cruisers were disposed as follows :

Inflexible (flag) and *Indefatigable* about 30 miles west of Marsala, Sicily, and the *Indomitable* had left Bizerta at 8 pm, after coaling, steering eastwards. That the destroyers were at Vasilico Bay, Santa Maura, seriously short of coal, and unable, therefore, to proceed at high speed to attack the *Goeben* at night.

9. That it therefore appeared that the accused would get no support for the First Cruiser Squadron, and that from his then position it was impossible for him to attack the *Goeben* before daylight.

10. That, in view of the instructions received, the accused was justified in considering that he must not abandon his watch on the Adriatic, having regard to the transportation of the French troops then taking place between Algeria and France, and the possibility of the Austrian fleet coming out.

11. That, in view of the instructions received from the Admiralty by the Commander-in-Chief and repeated by him in his sailing orders to the accused, and also the signal made on 4 August, viz., "First Cruiser Squadron and *Gloucester* are not to get seriously engaged with superior force", the Court are of opinion that, *under the particular circumstances of weather, time and position, the accused was justified* in considering the *Goeben* was a superior force to the First Cruiser Squadron at the time they would have met, viz., 6 am on 7 August, in full daylight in the open sea. (Author's italics.)

12. That, although it might have been possible to bring the *Goeben* to action off Cape Malea, or in the Cervi Channel, the Court considers that, in view of the accused's orders to keep a close watch on the Adriatic, he was justified in abandoning the chase at the time he did, as he had no news or prospect of any force being sent to his assistance.

13. The Court therefore finds that the charge against the

accused is not proved, and fully and honourably acquits him of the same.'

There remained one final act of justice : and for Troubridge —after his long-drawn-out ordeal, the social and professional slights, the newspaper lies—this was the supreme gesture of restitution. As the official record states simply :

'The President returned the accused his sword.'

15

Their Lordships' Displeasure ...and Other Reactions

'The aftermath makes unpleasant reading.' MARDER

THE finding of the Court was forwarded to the Admiralty on 9 November, 1914. In due course, about a month later, the Sea Lords set down their unenthusiastic reactions to its verdict.

By now Admiral of the Fleet Lord Fisher was back as First Sea Lord, and his minute was very brief—and wholly hostile (quite predictably) to Milne. Troubridge's name is not mentioned, and there is no reason to think that Fisher shared the general anger in Whitehall at his acquittal. He wrote:

'This most disastrous event of the escape of the *Goeben* and lamentable blow to British Naval prestige would never have occurred had Sir B. Milne been off Messina with the three Battle Cruisers [Fisher could not resist putting his adored battle cruisers in capitals!], even if short of coal—at the time *Goeben* was at Messina Harbour, for then the *Goeben* could not possibly have escaped.'

The Fourth Sea Lord (Captain Cecil Lambert) was more sweeping:

'It is probable that there is not much difference of opinion as to the incorrectness of the finding.

'After much consideration I feel quite certain that it will not be possible to draw a minute for publication to the fleet which will not form the subject for a deplorable controversy, the result of which must be most harmful.

'A great blunder has been committed. The officer thought to be responsible has been tried and "fully and honourably acquitted".

'It will be best to leave that officer and the finding where they stand.'

It is of some significance that the same week as these minutes were being written, the same men were writing their comments on the disaster, mentioned in Troubridge's defence, to the three 'Cressys'—and (apart from Battenberg, in the last week of his career) they accepted the implicit blame attached in that case by the Court of Inquiry to the Admiralty directives which led to that disaster.

Admiral Tudor, the Third Sea Lord, minuted on the case:

'The finding of the Court Martial appears to be correct on the evidence educed, but I am of opinion that its conclusions are wrong, both from the commonsense point of view, and technically.

'As regards the former, the instructions given to the Rear-Admiral that the First Cruiser Squadron and *Gloucester* were "not to get seriously engaged with a superior force", taken in conjunction with the fact that he was twice informed that the *Goeben* was his objective, must, or should, have conveyed to him that his Squadron was not considered an inferior force, and that he was expected to attack her.

'If he did not think so, he should have informed his Commander-in-Chief instead of—by various signals made to and intercepted by the latter—leaving the Commander-in-Chief under the impression that the Rear-Admiral intended to meet and engage the *Goeben* . . .

'The whole action of the Rear-Admiral contrasts most strangely with that of the Captain of *Gloucester*, who in spite of inferior speed and of vastly inferior power, clung tenaciously to the *Goeben* until twice ordered back.

'The finding of the Court Martial that the First Cruiser Squadron was an inferior force to the *Goeben* and *Breslau* appears to be founded on exaggerated Gunnery expert evidence combined with an omission to consider all the factors which bore on the case. [In fact Tudor was himself a gunnery specialist.]

'That the ships of the First Cruiser Squadron stood a chance of being severely punished during an engagement with the *Goeben* can be accepted, but that they could have been destroyed, or nearly destroyed, before the *Goeben* had expended all her 11-inch ammunition appears to be to be out of the question.'

The Second Sea Lord was Sir Frederick Hamilton, described as 'a rather lazy officer of no great distinction'. He was (to use a favourite expression of the First Lord's) distinctly 'vexed' at the acquittal. His hostile minute begins:

'The Court has been entirely led off the track by a clever lawyer.

'The case to be tried was the simple charge of not engaging the enemy when flying, and one would imagine that it would have been sufficient to prove that the armoured cruisers were in a position to engage and that they refused action.

'If the accused had based his defence on the fact that going further to the south would have made it possible for the *Goeben* to evade him, and that the *Goeben*'s commanding speed would have enabled her to get into the Adriatic without being engaged, it would have been difficult to say that he was not giving a good strategical excuse, but he did nothing of the sort, and entirely gave his case away by basing his defence on the supposed fact that he was an inferior force...

'Captain Wray makes out that if a ship is faster and has longer-range guns than the enemy's ships she is so immeasurably superior that no comparison is possible, in fact he

17. This unpublished letter (quoted on p. 26) is a good example of
Fisher's emphatic style

Confidential   14 Nov 1912

My dear Troubridge,

Your position on the list makes it impossible for me to offer you the position of 2nd in command in the Mediterranean; but I am g glad to be able to offer you the command of the Mediterranean cruisers. The Defence who is returning from China to exchange with the Hampshire will be available for your Flagship.

Yours sincerely,
Winston S. Churchill

18. Churchill writes in his own hand to appoint Troubridge to the
Mediterranean Command

represents it by 1/0 or infinity, and as, mathematically, infinity multiplied [or, more logically, 'divided'] by anything remains infinity, it follows that according to his argument the *Goeben* would have been superior to any number of *Defences*.

'It is a pity the Court did not test this monstrous argument by asking Captain Wray with how many *Defences* he would have considered himself justified in engaging the *Goeben* ...

'The Court however allowed themselves to be led away into trying the Commander-in-Chief for his disposition of the ships under his command, and so admitted a cloud of irrelevance to obscure the issue.

'By implication the Court appears to consider these dispositions were not good, but as they were not ordered to try the Commander-in-Chief it seems very unfair to judge him without letting him have an opportunity to defend himself.'

Hamilton's final paragraph sums up his conclusions:

'To take the paragraphs of the Finding in order:
Nos. 1 to 9 are matters of fact.
No. 10 is not concurred in, as the accused was twice told that *Goeben* was his objective.
No. 11 is not concurred in; the *Goeben* was not a superior force.
No. 12 is not concurred in; he was distinctly told the *Goeben* was his objective, and if he considered the order was incompatible with the former order to hold the entrance to the Adriatic, he should have pointed out the fact to the Commander-in-Chief.

'I am of opinion that nothing more should now be done in the matter, except that Captain Wray should remain unemployed, as it is decidedly dangerous to have an officer of his opinions in a responsible position.'

The last and most objective minute came from Admiral of the Fleet Sir Arthur Wilson VC—a remarkable man, holding an honourable but anomalous position at the Admiralty—lately

First Sea Lord, and now brought back as an unpaid adviser. Churchill has left us his assessment of Wilson—one of the supreme accolades ever conferred on a fighter: 'He was, without any exception, the most selfless man I have ever met or even read of.'

Sir Arthur summed up the salient facts, and continued:

'At 3.30 Captain Fawcet Wray went to him (Troubridge) and persuaded him that to attack would be suicide of the squadron and he gave up the chase.

'The whole question rests on whether the *Goeben* under the circumstances was a superior force to the First Cruiser Squadron and the *Dublin* and *Gloucester*.

'The two latter are not taken account of in the finding, although in the event of the *Goeben* chasing the cruiser squadron and just keeping out of range of its guns while within the range of her own, the *Dublin* and *Gloucester* would have had an excellent opportunity of closing and using their torpedoes.

'The *Goeben* could no doubt choose her own range but, unless the German gunnery is very much better than ours, she would have to expend all her ammunition before she could put the four ships out of action keeping outside 15,400 yards.'

This was a fair and most cogent comment, as one would expect from such a source.

'The Decision of the Court Martial has very little bearing on the escape of the ships, as nothing Admiral Troubridge could do, after the ships were once clear of the Straits of Messina, could prevent their escaping if they wished to do so without fighting, and our Battle Cruisers were too far away to take any part in the pursuit.

'*No one had foreseen at the time the effect of the ships making for the Dardanelles.* The other two contingencies, their making for the Adriatic or the Straits of Gibraltar, were provided for.'

(The passage here italicized is a most significant concession, and a typically forthright one; it came from a member of the tiny inner circle in ultimate authority at the Admiralty.)

There is apparently no final minute from Churchill; his earlier minute on Milne was a bleak single phrase: 'The explanation is satisfactory, the result unsatisfactory.'

But there were a number of striking reactions by others with special knowledge. Leslie Scott, whose brilliant defence had so nettled some of Their Lordships, told Admiral Fremantle after the trial: 'I expected an acquittal on the charge as framed; but if Troubridge had been tried for vacillation, no counsel could have saved him.'

Fremantle, himself a member of almost as distinguished a naval family as Troubridge, wrote long years later of the unpleasant duty of acting as Prosecutor:

'The facts were clear and the issue a very fine one. My own opinion was:

1. That the Admiralty telegram [the now notorious one of 30 July] was badly worded, and should have been restricted to stating the known facts and the relevant considerations, and should not have cramped the decision of the man on the spot, by giving him direct instructions as to whether or not to engage.

2. That Troubridge assumed too readily that the *Goeben* could steam at her full reputed speed, that her guns were in good order, that she had plenty of coal, and no anxiety as to replacing the large amount of ammunition which would inevitably be expended in long-range firing. He was also inclined to magnify the effect of the deficiencies, of which of course he had full knowledge, in his own ships. The *Goeben*'s destination was unknown, but it was evident that, whatever it was, she would have the power to do considerable damage to the Allied cause. Milne with his three battle cruisers was within 200 miles. [This was a very low estimate, since Milne was still at Malta.] Troubridge should have maintained his

original, and instinctive, decision to bring her to action at daylight, and hoped for the best. The *Goeben*, far from her home bases, could not have afforded the great expenditure of ammunition which is required in very long-range firing, so she would probably have closed to a range within that of the cruisers. Troubridge might well have expected to lose one or two ships, but he might also have expected to do the *Goeben* such damage as would make it possible for Milne with the battle cruisers to come up and finish her off. If the *Goeben* elected to use her superior speed to evade the Third Cruiser Squadron [he meant "First"] by steaming round them, at any rate some time would have been gained.

'An analogy is sometimes drawn between the *Goeben* incident and Cradock's action against von Spee, and I have heard it said by high authority that "if Troubridge had been where Cradock was and Cradock where Troubridge was, it is likely that more advantageous decisions would have been taken".[1]

This comment must be linked with another by Churchill in the same context. [Admiral Cradock's defeat by a squadron of cruisers, known for their crack gunnery, occurred in the same week as the Troubridge Court Martial.] The First Lord wrote to Beatty on 22 November, 1914, 'Steer mid-way between Troubridge and Cradock and all will be well, Cradock preferred.'

We know from Troubridge himself that his choice of action, or rather inaction, directly influenced Cradock in the crucial issue that cost him his life. Troubridge wrote, probably in 1925:

'I was informed by an officer of high rank [possibly Admiral Sir Hedworth Meux who had sat on the original Court of Enquiry] that in the last letter he received from my old friend Admiral Cradock he said, alluding to the fact that I was to be tried by Court Martial for not having engaged the *Goeben*, "I will take care not to suffer the fate of poor Troubridge." He engaged as all the world knows at Coronel under the most unfavourable circumstances possible and all his ships and men

[1] Fremantle, *My Naval Career*.

were destroyed by the enemy without any corresponding advantage whatever being gained.'

In 1916 a Memorial was unveiled to Cradock in York Minster. Its concluding lines run:

If our time be come, let us die manfully for our brethren,
And let us not stain our honour.

How eagerly Troubridge would have accepted such a fate and such an epitaph, if only he had turned a deaf ear to the defeatist warnings of a gunnery expert and had followed his own natural, combative instincts.

A letter exists from an admiral of another era, Collingwood. In 1808 he wrote:

'My heart was bent on the destruction of that fleet [the French admiral had slipped out of Corfu while Collingwood was at Syracuse, so the locations were fairly similar], but I never got intelligence where they really were until they were out of reach. Their escape was by chance; for at one time we were very near them without knowing it.'

These words of grief may well have been familiar to Troubridge who was widely read in naval history; and he came to know something of the same heart-break.

Vice-Admiral Sir David Beatty, commanding the battle cruiser squadron in northern waters, wrote bitterly to his wife, the recipient of so many confidences: 'To think that it is to the Navy to provide the first and only instance of failure. God, it makes me sick.'

But the ultimate verdict shall be Professor Marder's:

'The "ifs" will explain, but they cannot excuse. Instead of a smashing success which was easily within British grasp and which would have been of inestimable psychological, political, and strategic value at the beginning of the war, a bitter disappointment was the result. The escape of the *Goeben* was a blow to British naval prestige and naval morale.'

Finally, it may be fitting to refer here to the fate of some of the ships mentioned in connection with the *Goeben*.

The flagship *Inflexible* was placed under Admiral Sturdee's command in November and took part in the destruction of von Spee's squadron at the battle of the Falkland Islands on 8 December, 1914. During the main naval assault on the Dardanelles in March, 1915, *Inflexible* was severely damaged by a mine, being later towed to Malta for repairs.

At Jutland the involvement of Milne's ships was striking and tragic. Of the seven major units (ships of more than 10,000 tons) concerned with the pursuit of the *Goeben*, six were present on 31 May, 1916. Four of these—*Indefatigable*, *Defence*, *Black Prince* and *Warrior*—were sunk. (Captain Kennedy, who had been Senior Officer at the first encounter on 4 August, now found himself commanding Admiral Hood's Battle Cruiser Squadron.) Expressed another way, the measure of disaster is even more evident: there were forty-five major British units at Jutland, and six were lost; of these six, four had chased the *Goeben*.

The end of Troubridge's flagship, *Defence*, was one of the most horrendous episodes of the battle. Her admiral, Sir Robert Arbuthnot, was a famous fire-eater. He had long declared his intention of taking up his assigned flank position, after formal deployment, by the shortest route, no matter if this carried him between two opposing lines of heavy ships already in action. This, in fact, was what he did at the crisis of the battle, though low mist concealed the enemy till he was a mere 8,000 yards away. Five German capital ships instantly saw *Defence* and smothered her with fire; she 'suddenly disappeared completely in an immense column of smoke and flame, hundreds of feet high. It appeared to be an absolutely instantaneous destruction, the ship seeming to be dismembered at once.' There were no survivors. Her sister ship, *Warrior*, vanished in the same maelstrom and by midnight the third of Troubridge's original four armoured cruisers, *Black Prince*, had gone.

These disasters raise the question, largely ignored at the Court Martial, of comparative strength of armour. After Jutland it was painfully clear that 'armoured' cruisers carried unduly light protection and thus were extremely vulnerable to the gunfire of heavy ships.

16

Black Sea and Aegean

'The happy delusion that there were sufficient brains.'
ADMIRAL WEMYSS, FIRST SEA LORD

HISTORIANS will long debate the likely nature and timing of the Turkish role if Souchon had failed. All that concerns us here are the indisputable results of his success.

The premature bombardment of the Gallipoli peninsula ordered by the Admiralty and carried out on 3 November lasted only ten minutes; but its effects were prolonged and, to the attackers, costly in the extreme. The Turks could not fail to foresee the general strategy of the Allies, and set about strengthening the Dardanelles forts and minefields. Virtually all traffic through the Straits ceased for four years, apart from some intrepid submariners, whose exploits were among the most outstanding of the war. But the great objectives of frightening the Turks into neutrality, maintaining a lifeline of supplies to Russian Black Sea ports, and attacking the enemy through the Balkans, were totally frustrated.

An unintentional product of our failure in 1914 was the unforeseen, and indeed incredible, stiffening of Turkish resistance. On the British side, what Churchill called, with understandable bitterness, 'an insurmountable mental barrier', reinforced the defences of the Dardanelles.

'A wall of crystal, utterly immovable, began to tower up in the Narrows, and against this wall of inhibition no weapon

could be employed. The "No" principle had become estab-
lished.[1]

No such inhibitions troubled the Turks. It is often implied that
the head of the German Military Mission, General Liman von
Sanders, dominated the Turkish armed forces. This is less than
the truth. Although there were eventually as many as 25,000
German officers and men in the Ottoman empire by the end of
the war, 'the Ottoman armed forces remained exclusively an
instrument of Turkish policy'.[2]

The future hero of Turkish arms and of the nation was a
mere Lieutenant Colonel, Mustapha Kemal, temporarily commanding a division under Liman; but he proved a superlative
field commander.

The Gallipoli campaign lies outside our story. Only the briefest
commentary is necessary. Neither Lord Fisher nor Kitchener were
wholly and consistently committed to the Dardanelles. The latter
acted not merely as Secretary of State but Chief-of-Staff (in all
but name), and Churchill was to tell the Dardanelles Com-
mission, after Kitchener had been drowned in June, 1916 on
his way to Russia :

'When he gave a decision it was invariably accepted as final.
He was never, to my belief, overruled by the War Council or
the Cabinet in any military matter, great or small . . . Scarcely
anyone ever ventured to argue with him in Council . . . All-
powerful, imperturbable, reserved, he dominated absolutely
our councils at this time.'[3]

The effect on Turkish morale, a potentially powerful, though
unpredictable, quality, of the glittering and menacing German
warships anchored off the Golden Horn is easy to guess. To
acquire such magnificent allies would have raised the spirits of
a far less unsophisticated populace.

If these two ships in Turkish waters led, directly or indirectly,

[1] *The World Crisis.*
[2] Ulrich Trumpener, *Germany and the Ottoman Empire.*
[3] *The World Crisis.*

to the Gallipoli campaign, the cost in blood was staggering—an outcome where mere figures have virtually lost their meaning, in terms of human suffering. The casualties in the Dardanelles struggle were:

British losses: 205,000
French losses: 47,000
Turkish losses: 251,000 (this official figure has unofficially been put as high as 350,000).

In this context there is one summary that is irresistible. John Masefield, serving in a hospital ship near the Dardanelles, wrote with the realistic eye of a romantic poet, and conveyed something of the Turkish viewpoint. If to-day his words sound to our dulled ears unduly dramatic, it must be remembered that they were written at white heat very soon after the final evacuation, and were coloured by Masefield's own bitter experience.

'"Still," our enemies say, "you did not win the Peninsula." We did not; and some day, when truth will walk clear-eyed, it will be known why we did not. Until then, let our enemies say this: "They did not win, but they came across three thousand miles of sea, a little Army without reserves and short of munitions, a band of brothers, not half of them half-trained, and nearly all of them new to war. They came to what we said was an impregnable fort,... and by sheer naked manhood they beat us, and drove us out of it. Then, rallying, but without reserves, they beat us again, and drove us farther. Then rallying once more, but still without reserves, they beat us again, this time to our knees. Then, had they had reserves, they would have conquered, but by God's pity they had none. Then, after a lapse of time, when we were men again, they had reserves, and they hit us a staggering blow, which needed but a push to end us, but God again had pity. After that our God was indeed pitiful, for England made no further thrust, and they went away." '4

4 John Masefield, *Gallipoli*.

But to return to the direct effects of the *Goeben* and *Breslau* based on the Bosphorous: their presence offered two major benefits to the Turks. Firstly, they conducted a series of elusive but damaging raids on the fairly ineffectual Russian fleet in the Black Sea. Secondly, their presence was an unceasing threat to British and Allied naval control in the Eastern Mediterranean.

The aggressive actions under Souchon were varied in scope and fortune. The ships, though notionally Turkish, and wearing the star and crescent Ottoman flag, were essentially crewed by Germans, and the few Turkish ships that went with them were alleged always to have effective supervising German officers on board.

As has been mentioned, Souchon's first effort was by far his most important. The shelling of Russian ports on 29 October did much material damage—but, of far greater moment, it made war with Russia certain.

A wireless rating in the *Goeben* has left an eye-witness account of the attack on Sevastopol. The Germans alleged that the Russians had already laid mines in neutral waters near the Bosphorus, and that a crushing reprisal was appropriate. It was certainly carried out eagerly. For twenty-five minutes at a range of as little as 4,000 yards the heavy bombardment with ten 11-inch guns continued. The numerous fortress guns on shore fired back. Sevastopol was a heavily armed base. There were a number of near-misses, but *Goeben* turned away intact. It was after the range had opened to 10 miles that a fresh shore salvo scored two hits, but the damage was minimal.

As they steamed for home, the *Goeben* picked up Russian messages *en clair* telling of minelaying in her path. The minelayer was spotted in the very act. With unusual humanity the Germans ordered the Russian vessel to stop and lower boats. This was done and no lives were lost—with one exception. This was the ship's chaplain who decided to go down with his ship. This act was, perhaps, worthy of General Bosquet's classic comment at Balaclava—('*C'est magnifique...*').

At the same time the *Breslau* was engaged in attacking the

oil installations at Novorossisk, beyond the Crimea. The results were spectacular and the photographs remind one of similar exploits in a later war. Meanwhile Turkish destroyers caused damage to Odessa.

A young sailor in the *Goeben* wrote, 'It had all happened so quickly that the diplomats had not kept pace with it. They were now faced with accomplished facts.' This was the simple truth.

The crew continued the provocative farce of wearing the fez in Constantinople. A familiar order on returning to harbour, which grew to have pleasant associations, concerned the restoration of their crumpled headgear. There was a special local technique by which the fez was pressed between two heated brass blocks. So in harbour came the routine order : 'Iron fezzes.'

In November, 1914, just off Balaclava in thick fog, *Goeben* ran into the main Russian fleet, including six capital ships. Apparently the Russians had laid a trap with success, and when the *Goeben* was suddenly visible (though she was still unaware of the enemy), the Russians opened fire at about 4,000 yards. *Breslau* wisely took refuge under the lee of the *Goeben*, which was struck by a 12-inch shell and suffered many casualties. The Germans returned the enemy fire, scored some hits on the battleship, *St Ewstasi*, and withdrew, still half-hidden in the coastal fog-bank. The Russians declined to pursue them.

A major incident occurred on 26 December, 1914. As *Goeben* was returning towards the Bosphorus she struck a mine on the starboard side, which blew a hole 64 square metres in size. The ship took on a heavy list, and appeared doomed. But shortly came a second explosion. By good fortune this second mine had struck the port side, and slowly the ship, though alarmingly deep in the water, returned to an even keel. By chance a senior German general was on board, Field Marshal Freiherr von der Goltz, who held a somewhat anomalous position. Liman, who was nothing if not prickly, found his presence a trifle embarrassing. Goltz had the bad luck to die a little later—from spotted fever.

As the Gallipoli campaign developed, some ratings from *Goeben* were formed into a machine-gun detachment and sent to join the army, and two of her 5.9-inch guns were dismounted and transported to serve on land as field guns.

The problem of repairing the two huge holes without a dry-dock was solved by constructing two coffer dams; these had to be on an enormous scale, and weighed 354 tons. But during this slow process she was needed so urgently that she jettisoned the coffer dams and, relying on her bulkheads, steamed slowly out into the Black Sea. The urgency stemmed from the plight of a Turkish cruiser about to be overtaken by Russian ships. Later it was learned that the Russians had turned for home; apparently Allied spies in Constantinople had reported the heavy black smoke, which the *Goeben* was making in her efforts to get quickly to sea, and had sent out warning signals.

Before the repair work was complete, news came on 18 March that the Allies were attempting to force the Narrows. There was clearly a strong chance of success—and this left the Turks with no doubt that Constantinople would swiftly fall. Among the crew there was a rumour that *Goeben* had been ordered to raise steam, and approach the Eastern end of the Dardanelles. If the Allies broke through, the alleged orders were: 'Fight to the death!' But by 6 pm it was known that the Allied assault had failed and the *Goeben* was reprieved.

In fact, the *Goeben* and *Breslau* took no direct part in the Gallipoli campaign, since no Allied surface ship ever penetrated the Narrows. However, a legend has grown up, based on no less an authority than Sir Julian Corbett, supported by Admiral Lord Keyes (then Commodore and Chief of Staff) that *Goeben* made an appearance and joined in the firing against the Allied positions on the Peninsula.

This is not so; and the witnesses on whose reports Corbett relied must have confused the *Goeben* with lesser ships.

The facts, fully documented by the Official German History, are these: Souchon was anxious to use the maximum fire-power across the Peninsula, and he proposed to add the *Goeben* to his other battleships. Early on 2 May he sailed from Constantinople, hoping to arrive at daybreak the next day, open fire without warning, and return before the enemy got the range. However, shortly after sailing, a telegram arrived from Admiral von Usedom, commanding the special section of the land defences manned by sailors (the *Sonderkommando Usedom*), warning him that owing to the Allied use of observation balloons, the method of fire control hitherto in use by the Germans was no longer suitable, and advising that he return to the Bosphorus. Thus it is clear, beyond doubt, that *Goeben* never came within 100 miles of participation in the main battle for Gallipoli.[5]

Clearly Allied observers assumed that they were seeing *Goeben*'s massive and individual outline instead of the ancient Turkish ships that were engaged in bombardment. But seen from the air a ship may not present the standard naval silhouette; and the soldiers under fire would believe that any 11-inch shell fragments must be from *Goeben*'s guns.

On 10 May, the Russians set a trap with considerable cunning, using a single ship, the *Kagul*, to give the impression that a landing was planned 150 miles from the Bosphorus on the south coast of the Black Sea. When the *Goeben* arrived, short of coal, having been interrupted in coaling, she found that the Russian forces had seemingly gone. Later the *Kagul* was seen moving towards the Bosphorus. The *Goeben* chased her—only to find a large squadron including six battleships lying in wait, not under way, and partly screened by mist. The tactical dispositions were well planned, as the *Kagul* on the flank could spot the fall of shot and report to her fleet. At a range estimated at 15,000 yards the duel continued for half an hour. *Goeben* was twice hit with 12-inch shells. The position was unfavourable, with fuel shortage a main factor. As a bluff, *Goeben* set course as if for Sevastopol. There were seventeen warships in all in pursuit.

When *Goeben* began to turn, the Russians elected to turn 'in succession'. This tactic diminished their chance of a crushing

[5] Hans von Mohl, who was Navigating Officer of SMS *Breslau* in 1914, and later served on Souchon's staff, confirms that neither German ship took part in the bombardment of the Gallipoli beaches. (Letter to author dated 7 May, 1973.)

victory. For the *Goeben* there was little point in continued firing (and on this occasion her standard of gunnery was to earn official criticism); but for some reason the Russians also held their fire, while the *Goeben* at full steam maintained a wide turn ahead of the pursuing enemy. Gradually, using her still remarkable turn of speed, she drew out of range—and another 'escape' could be added to her strange and lonely record.

One of *Goeben*'s crew has told of another encounter in the Black Sea in September, 1916. (For some reason there is no reference to this in the official history.) It began as a routine sweep in fine weather. Suddenly, under a cloudless sky, she came under heavy fire at extreme range, estimated at about 15 miles. Her opponent was the new Russian superdreadnought, *Imperatriza Maria*, of 22,500 tons. She was outside *Goeben*'s range, but came close to straddling *Goeben*—the precise converse of what Troubridge had avoided. The Russian battleship was reputed to have a speed of 25 knots, and direct escape was probably not feasible. *Goeben* had acquired a seaplane, and it was hoped that her bombs would confuse or delay the enemy, and prevent the range being closed. After a long interval there was still no sign of the returning seaplane. Then, at last, it was found drifting helpless, dead ahead. Using a tackle fixed near the muzzle of a laterally mounted gun, the plane was snatched from the water, while the enemy was starting to overhaul *Goeben*—an unfamiliar experience for her confident crew. In spite of stopping to rescue her airmen, however, she made good her escape. On 22 July, while *Goeben* was under repair, *Breslau* also had a narrow escape, at extreme range, from *Imperatriza Maria*, but escaped with a splinter-scarred bow. By chance the dominant role of the *Imperatriza Maria* soon came to an abrupt end with an internal explosion at Sevastopol.

All these relatively minor naval skirmishes have remained little known. In January, 1918, a very different situation arose. The armistice with Russia (15 December, 1917) had deprived the Germans of any excuse for these Black Sea sorties. In London there had just been a wholesale reorganization at the Admiralty, and, inevitably, great hopes of brilliant new solutions and triumphs were aired. Sir Rosslyn Wemyss, who looked the part, elegant, urbane and effective, was First Sea Lord—replacing Jellicoe, by now a very tired and sorely tried leader. His political boss was Sir Eric Geddes, a ruthless and largely unwelcome successor to the friendly Carson. The Rear-Admiral Command-ing Aegean Squadron had, until recently, been Troubridge's prosecutor, Admiral Fremantle, a competent and efficient com-mander. But on 12 January, he was brought home to take up a high staff position at the Admiralty.

One of his main pre-occupations had been to deal with any breakout, however belated, by the *Goeben* or *Breslau*. Fremantle set out their likely objectives—if they did in fact make a sortie.

(1) To effect a junction with the Austrians in the Adriatic.

(2) A raid on our transport routes, returning to the Dar-danelles or to Smyrna.

(3) Attack on our bases at Mudros, or Salonika, or possibly Port Said or Alexandria.

Of these alternatives:

(1) Is considered to be the least unlikely, and to have a fair prospect of success.

(2) Is possible, but the chances of success would seem to be insufficient to warrant the risk incurred.

(3) Would be a desperate venture, which could only end in the eventual destruction of the enemy, and is conceivable only as a last resort, which might be decided upon in the event of Turkey determining a separate peace.

But, it was the 'desperate venture' on which the Germans were to build their hopes. An elaborate system of look-out stations was set up, and daily reconnaissance was carried out from the naval air base on Imbros. Apart from destroyer patrols, two pre-dreadnought (1904) battleships were kept at Mudros, able to raise steam in an hour. These were slow ships, but it was guessed that *Goeben* and *Breslau* could only muster 20 knots in company.

The exit from the Straits had been extensively mined, and it seemed certain that the Germans would be sure to sweep a channel before their most important ships were committed.

But not for the first time in the Mediterranean—whether with Milne in 1914 or in 1915 when Vice-Admiral Carden, the Admiral Superintendent Malta Dockyard, was suddenly placed in charge of the naval assault on the Narrows, 'a chivalry which surely outstripped common sense'—the wrong man was chosen to lead. Fremantle's successor was Rear-Admiral Hayes Sadler. Like Carden before him his health was clearly on the verge of collapsing under heavy responsibilities. A yacht, the *Triad*, was allocated to the admiral to take him on his many duty visits, necessary in covering a widely dispersed command. On 16 January, only four days after taking over his new duties, he decided that, as the *Triad* was not available for a visit to Salonika, he would take one of the two battleships, the *Lord Nelson*. This left the *Agamemnon* unsupported by her sister ship, in a situation where it was painfully obvious to all but Hayes Sadler that they should operate as a pair. In the event it may not have made a lot of difference to the outcome, but it certainly gave the Germans encouragement for their sortie, as they were well informed that only one battleship was available at Mudros.

By 20 January the squadron remained dangerously dispersed; in all there were about thirty-five vessels, some at Mudros harbour in the island of Lemnos, some at Crete, some at Salonika and some at Imbros, the largest island near the Narrows.

Fremantle's orders were in part precise and positive, and naturally the new admiral had not had time to modify them, even if he had the mind. These orders recognized that it would be madness for the two ancient battleships to attempt solo heroics, since 'the primary consideration is to destroy the enemy. This is best attained not by attack regardless of circumstances, but by leading him in a direction in which support may be obtained, and where he can be brought to action by superior force.' These last two words, which have had to recur so often in this narrative, must have been burned into Fremantle's mind forever during the Troubridge Court Martial. However, the operative signal, due to be made if the Germans threatened to emerge, was unduly blunt: 'Take all necessary action to engage the enemy.'

As the Official Historian, Sir Henry Newbolt, commented: 'This was an order which Britsh naval officers could only interpret in one way.' So the men on the spot, the captains of the thirty-five ships which might be involved, were once again left with a muddled directive. Souchon, the *Goebenadmiral* as his biographer had called him, was no longer the senior commander. Vice-Admiral von Rebeur-Paschwitz, his successor, could not endure the prospect of his two potentially menacing ships being confined to the Bosphorus. The Turks had just lost Jerusalem and a dramatic naval victory might raise their sagging morale.

A plan of exceptional boldness was evolved. The general aim was to sink the small vessels patrolling the outlet of the Dardanelles; then, while the *Breslau* kept watch nearby, the *Goeben* would bombard Mudros (on the south side of Lemnos). Even a battleship at anchor would be (like the French Fleet at Oran in 1940) at a terrible disadvantage. The German light escort of four destroyers would turn back at the west end of the Straits, but a German U-boat would lay mines off Mudros.

The allied defensive plans were at first ineffective. The two British destroyers failed to sight the enemy and their movements were governed by the position of the British minefields. The nearest point to the Straits available to the Allies was Mavro island, nine miles distant from Cape Helles. The look-outs there saw nothing, owing to a thick dawn mist. It was six o'clock in the morning.

The German ships set course first west and then south-west. The German admiral seems to have been at little pains to discover in advance where the Allied mines were laid. At 6.10 am the *Goeben* struck a mine, but there was only slight damage. So she turned north towards Imbros and ordered *Breslau* to control the situation to the north of the island. *Breslau* dispersed

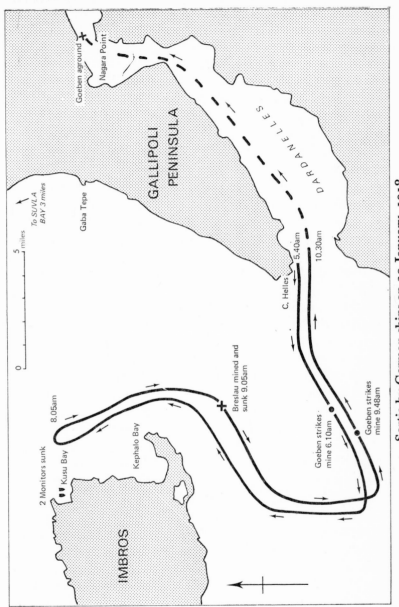

Sortie by German ships on 20 January, 1918.

the two destroyers, *Lizard* and *Tigress*, and the *Goeben* sank the two monitors, *Lord Raglan* and *M28*, at anchor in Kusu Bay at the north-east corner of Imbros. Admiral von Rebeur-Paschwitz then decided to turn south, following the same course he had used for the outward run, which he assumed was free of mines. He could then set about the highly dangerous business of bombarding Mudros harbour. But there were now bombers attacking his ships. *Breslau* moved out of line, in theory to give *Goeben* better scope for anti-aircraft fire, and in so doing struck a mine. It was in fact at the extreme limit of the minefield guarding Imbros. Suddenly the situation was disastrously out of control. The *Goeben* attempted to take the *Breslau* in tow, and struck a mine herself; the air attack continued, and *Breslau* was hit by a bomb; the Germans could see mines all around them; anxious lookouts reported a submarine; the *Tigress* and *Lizard* were fulfilling their proper function of turning on their pursuer, and within thirty-five minutes of this triple concentration of air, sea and underwater forces, *Breslau* sank.

The German Official History is sharply critical on one single issue—the fatal manoeuvre that took the *Breslau* wide of the *Goeben*'s course, especially as the latter's compass had been put out of action by the earlier mining.

Now the Germans had only one course left—to retreat at full speed for the comparative security of the Straits. There was in fact no chance of pursuit by battleship, even if Hayes Sadler had had the prudence to leave them together. *Goeben* aimed to circumvent the many minefields by a wide sweep to the south, following her outward track. But her luck had run out. At 9.48 am she struck a second mine close to the scene of the first. Still she was able to maintain an adequate speed, listing badly and undamaged this time by another heavy bombing attack. At last with safety in sight, she ran on to a sandbank as she passed Nagara, the south-western point of the Sea of Marmora, near the inner entrance to the Straits.

There seemed no chance of floating her off, and for six days she remained a stationary target for further onslaughts by bombers. A total of 270 sorties—a large number for those days—were flown for this purpose. But though fixed on the sand, she was far from disarmed, and accurate anti-aircraft fire aided by poor weather prevented any serious damage. There were two hits, but the small bombs then in use would never have put her out of action.

Attempts were made with seaplanes to torpedo her, but they were too late. A monitor was brought up to shoot at her across the Gallipoli Peninsula—but to no avail. Then it was the turn of the British submarines, whose service had gained so enviable a reputation for skill and gallantry in 1915. E-12, though handicapped by a fractured driving shaft but able to work both propellors by electricity, volunteered to launch an attack (having of course first to traverse the mined approaches)—but her captain was forbidden to do so. Two other submarines, ordered from Corfu and Malta, arrived—only to find that Hayes Sadler was unwilling to let them take the risk either. He hoped that Gough-Calthorpe, the Commander-in-Chief, would arrive to 'carry the can'. Eventually he did and E-14 sailed a week after the *Goeben* had been grounded—only to find that the bird had flown. Alas, the gallant E-14 was lost on the return journey. A third submarine, E-2, was commanded by Lieutenant Bonham-Carter; his First Lieutenant told Professor Marder (whose account of this largely forgotten episode remains the fullest and most vivid) that he

'remembers vividly Bonham-Carter's air of contempt and exasperation when he returned from discussing with Hayes Sadler whether we should have a shot at the *Goeben*—refusing to take any responsibility or allow it to others, and with a pipe in his mouth all the time down which he dribbled! It seems he was waiting for the arrival of Gough-Calthorpe to make the decision.'

The courage and quality of these First World War submariners in their primitive craft in heavily mined straits, their progress harassed by steel nets, and complicated by unusual problems of stability in swirling waters of unequal density, cannot be exaggerated.

After a week of frantic effort, the task of refloating the *Goeben* seemed hopeless. Then, by an unusual device, the old Turkish battleship *Turget Reis* was warped securely alongside the stranded ship, and she stirred the sandbank by varied action of her screws. This eventually broke the suction effect, and *Goeben* was towed off—and so back to Constantinople,[6] where morale, already shaky, was gravely upset by the loss of the *Breslau*.

For *Goeben* the war was over but unfortunately this could not be known with certainty to the Aegean command. There was natural anxiety that next time she might emerge to block the Suez Canal. So again she posed a threat, imaginary but undeniable, which occupied numbers of ships with their crews at a time when the convoys needed all the escorts available.

The First Sea Lord's pungent comment contrasted sharply with his usual urbane approach :

'The *Goeben* getting away is perfectly damnable and has considerably upset me, since we at the Admiralty were under the happy delusion that there were sufficient brains and sufficient means out there to prevent it : of the latter there were; of the former, apparently not.'

Poor indecisive Hayes Sadler was relieved of his command. A kindly historian has noted that he was a sick man. However, he survived the bungled operation to achieve the ripe age of eighty-nine.

Anger at home at the muddle would have been less, had it not involved the very ship that had been so sharp a thorn in the Navy's flesh in 1914. *The Times* reminded its readers that 'the story of their escape from Messina represents one of the greatest of our blunders'.

[6] Air Marshal Sir Ralph Sorley recalls being sent on a hazardous reconnaissance and finding that the missing *Goeben* was back at Constantinople.

The Eastern Mediterranean in those testing days had not always attracted the best of leadership.

But twenty-two years later the great tradition of naval mastery was renewed under the matchless leadership of Cunningham and Vian and with the superlative support of the fleet.

It was *they* who, in desperate circumstances and at fearful cost, accepted every challenge, and achieved in these waters fresh honours for the Royal Navy.

Epilogue. Yavuz at Peace

A T the end of the war, the fiction that *Goeben-Yavus* was a Turkish ship became an actuality. She was formally handed over to the Turks, a generous treaty provision in marked contrast to the confiscation and internment of the German High Seas Fleet.

The formidable task of repairing and refitting her occupied a very long time, and it was as late as March, 1930, that she finally reappeared off Constantinople, fully modernized and ready for her sea trials. These were successful and the Ottoman Navy were now the proud owners of a modern battle cruiser. She had been renamed *Yavuz Sultan Selim*. 'Yavuz' is the Turkish for 'terrible' or 'inflexible'—so her name was the equivalent of 'Sultan Selim the Terrible', in honour of one of Turkey's greatest leaders.

Her early post-war condition had been so serious that she was anchored in the shallow waters of the Gulf of Izmit; the idea was that, if her bulkheads collapsed, she would touch the bottom before being submerged.

Later, in her reconditioned form, she looked magnificent, at least to outward appearances; and this spick and span state was rigorously maintained as a fairly recent photograph shows.

In 1966, a matter of fifty-five years after she was launched in Hamburg, she was offered for sale. Surprisingly, it was in the *New York Herald Tribune* that an advertisement appeared as follows : 'The battle cruiser *Yavuz* has completed her service. She is 22,350 tons unladen. Estimated price about $2,800,000.' At that date offers did not reach that price, and she remained with Turkey. The national press extolled her past exploits, and what was called 'her epic fame' was recalled. She was, they said, a fine combination of glamour and power. There were patriotic references to the last salute to her ensign on Atatürk's quarterdeck, 'before she went to her eternal repose'.

But the irrevocable step towards the breakers' yard has been deferred from month to month; and like some unhappy prisoner awaiting his long-postponed doom in 'death row', she lingers on, still afloat, at the Naval Base at Gölcük—in the remotest corner of the Marmora, 40 miles from Istanbul. She has been described as recently as July, 1972, by a visiting historian, Mr Peter Liddle, as 'still majestic in her sadly moribund decay like a gasping, stranded whale'.

Political affinities have undergone vast changes and abrupt reversals since her early exploits. Turkey and Britain have for years been friendly allies. But in this country *Goeben* will not soon be forgotten. She earned for our former enemies great glory; for us she is best recalled in Churchill's striking epitaph: in 1914 she had carried with her, he said, 'for the peoples of the East and Middle East more slaughter, more misery and more ruin than has ever been borne within the compass of a ship'.

BIBLIOGRAPHY

Principal sources

Churchill, W. S., *The World Crisis*, revised single volume edition, Butterworth, 1931

Fremantle, Adm Sir Sydney, *My Naval Career*, Hutchinson, 1949

Kopp, Georg, *Two Lone Ships*, Hutchinson, 1931

Lumby, E. W. R. (Ed) (The Navy Records Society), *The Mediterranean 1912–14*, 1970

Marder, Arthur J., *From the Dreadnought to Scapa Flow*, Vols I–V, OUP, 1961–70

Marder, Arthur J., *Fear God and Dread Nought*, Vols II–III, Cape, 1956–8

Souchon, Rear-Adm W., *La Percée de SMS 'Goeben' et 'Breslau' de Messine aux Dardanelles*, Payot, 1930

Other sources

Asquith, H. H., *Memories and Reflections*, Cassell, 1928

Beresford, Adm Lord, *Memoirs*, Methuen, 1914

Buchan, John, *The King's Grace*, Hodder, 1935

Chalmers, Rear-Admiral W. S., *The Life and Letters of David Beatty*, Hodder & Stoughton, 1951.

Churchill, W. S., *My Early Life*, Macmillan, 1930

Churchill, Randolph S., *Winston S. Churchill*, Vol II, Heinemann, 1967, and Gilbert, Martin, Vol III, 1971

Corbett, Sir Julian, and Newbolt, Sir Henry, *The War at Sea*, Vols I–V, Longmans, 1920–31

Cunningham of Hyndhope, Admiral of the Fleet Viscount, *A Sailor's Odyssey*, Hutchinson, 1951.

Dewar, Vice-Adm K. G. B., *The Navy from Within*, Gollancz, 1939

Hough, Richard, *The Big Battleship*, Michael Joseph, 1966
James, Adm Sir William, *The Eyes of the Navy*, Methuen, 1955
Jane, Fred, *Fighting Ships*, 1914 edition
Jellicoe Papers, The Navy Records Society (Ed: Patterson). Vol I, 1966
Jenkins, Roy, *Asquith*, Collins, 1964
King-Hall, Cdr Sir Stephen, *My Naval Life*, Faber, 1952
Liddell Hart, Sir Basil, *T. E. Lawrence to his Biographer*, Cape, 1963.
Liman von Sanders, *Five Years in Turkey*, US Naval Institute, 1919
Longford, Elizabeth, *Wellington*, Vol II, Weidenfeld & Nicolson, 1972
Lorey, Rear-Adm Hermann, *Der Krieg in den türkischen Gewässern*, Vol I, Die Mittelmeer-Division, 1928, German Ministry of Marine (English translation in MS in Naval Library)
Lowis, G. L., *Fabulous Admirals*, Putnam, 1957
Mäkelä, M. E., *Souchon der Goebenadmiral*, Braunschweig
Marder, Arthur J., *Portrait of an Admiral*, Cape, 1952
Masefield, John, *Gallipoli*, Heinemann, 1916
Milne, Adm Sir Berkeley, *The Escape of the Goeben and Breslau*, Eveleigh Nash, 1921
Morganthau, Henry, *Secrets of the Bosphorus*, Hutchinson, 1918
Naval Staff Monographs (Historical), *The Mediterranean 1914–15* (1923), *The Naval Staff of the Admiralty* (1929)
Nicolson, Sir Harold, *Some People*, Constable, 1927
Trumpener, Ulrich, *Germany and the Ottoman Empire, 1914–18*, Princeton, 1968
Tuchman, Barbara, *August 1914*, Constable, 1962
The Dictionary of National Biography, OUP

Unpublished (manuscript) sources.

Troubridge Papers, National Maritime Museum
Milne Papers, National Maritime Museum
Personal Letters from Survivors.

INDEX

The basic ranks and titles of the main characters are those held in 1914. Personal dates have been included, if only as a tribute to the striking longevity of senior naval officers.

Grey, Sir Edward—*continued*
Viscount Grey of Falloden) (1862–1933), 12, 13, 43

Haldane, Viscount (1856–1928), 9, 15
Hall, Captain (later Admiral Sir) Reginald (1870–1943), 23, 46, 91
Hamilton, Admiral Sir Frederick (1856–1917), 21, 148–9
Hamilton, General Sir Ian (1853–1947), 30
Hankey, Captain Maurice (later Lord Hankey) (1877–1963), 48
Harwood, Commodore (later Admiral Sir) Henry (1888–1950), 96
Haus, Admiral (Austrian Commander-in-Chief), 67
Hayes-Sadler, Rear-Admiral Arthur (1863–1952), 165, 168–70
Hellespont, 85
Herbert, (Sir) A. P. (1890–1971), 114
Hood, Rear-Admiral the Hon. Sir Horace (1870–1916), 103, 154

Imbros, 85, 164–5, 168
Imperatriza Maria (Russian warship), 163
Indefatigable, HMS, xi, 47–8, 49, 58–9, 143–4, 154
Indomitable, HMS, xi, 47–8, 49, 58, 60, 98, 101, 143–4
Inflexible, HMS, 47–8, 58, 74, 138, 144, 154
Invincible, HMS, 5
Ireland, 11, 12
Isaacs, Sir Rufus (later 1st Marquess of Reading) (1860–1935), 114
Italy, 11, 33, 34, 35, 54, 100, 127
Italian Navy, 127

James, Commander (later Admiral Sir) William (1881–1973), 10, 84
Jellicoe, Admiral Sir John (later Admiral of the Fleet Earl Jellicoe) (1859–1935), 10, 91, 98, 99, 109, 166
Jerusalem, 166
Johnson, Sir Henry, 114
Jutland, Battle of, 154–5

Kagul (Russian warship), 162
Kelly, Captain (later Admiral Sir Howard) (1873–1952), 10, 70–1, 80–2
Kelly, Captain (later Admiral of the Fleet Sir) John (1871–1936), 10, 75, 82
Kennedy, Captain F. W., 58, 154
Keyes, Commodore (later Admiral of the Fleet Lord Keyes) (1872–1945), 10, 161
Kiel Canal, 6
King Edward VII, HMS, 95
King-Hall, Commander (later Lord King-Hall) (1893–1966), 9
Kitchener of Khartoum, Field-Marshal Earl (1850–1916), 157
Kress, Colonel Friedrich von, 84–5

Lambert, Captain (later Admiral Sir) Cecil (1864–1928), 146–7
Lapeyrère, Vice-Admiral Boué (1852–1924), 131
Lawrence, T. E. (1888–1935), 44
Lemnos, 164–7
Liddle, Peter, 173
Limpus, Rear-Admiral (Sir) Arthur (1863–1931), 35–7, 43
Lion, HMS, 110
Lizard, HMS, 168
Lloyd George, David (later 1st Earl Lloyd-George of Dwyfor) (1863–1945), 8, 39
Lord Nelson, HMS, 165
Lord Raglan (monitor), 168

M. 28 (monitor), 168
McKenna, Reginald (1863–1943), 15, 27, 30
Mackenzie, Sir Compton (1883–1972), 39
Mahan, Rear-Admiral A. T. (1840–1914), 17
Mallet, Sir Louis (1864–1936), 42, 44
Malta, 49, 50, 65, 74, 78, 100, 103, 127, 151
Marmora, Sea of, 106, 168
Marder, Professor Arthur J. (1910–), 1, 15, 17, 19, 22, 80, 146, 153–4, 169
Marston, Commander Guy, 114
Masefield, John (later Poet Laureate) (1878–1967), 158
Mavro Island, 166
May, Admiral of the Fleet Sir William (1849–1930), 25
Mediterranean Sea, *passim*
Messina (Straits of), xi, xii, 45, 49, 51, 54–5, 57–8, 63, 65, 67, 97, 100, 119, 131, 133, 137, 143, 146, 170
Meux, Admiral of the Fleet Sir Hedworth (1856–1929), 76, 94, 109, 152
Midilli (ex *Breslau*), 87
Milne, Admiral Sir Berkeley, 2nd Baronet (1855–1938), character, career and appearance, 24–8; prewar preparations, 49; dispositions on

ADRIATIC SEA

ITALY

ALB

Otranto

Pola 450 miles

CORFU

Goeben & Breslau

Troubridge
1st Cruiser Squadron

Milne Battle Cruisers

Dublin

IONIAN
SEA

12.08am A
1st C.S. (Troubridg

Goeben and Breslau pursued
by Gloucester

4.15

Palermo

Messina

5pm Aug. 6

Dublin

Midnight
Aug. 8

Au

SICILY

1am Aug. 7

Milne
(Battle Cruisers)

MALTA   Aug. 8